Other Letters to Milena / Otras cartas a Milena

Reina María Rodríguez

Other Letters to Milena / Otras cartas a Milena

Translated by Kristin Dykstra

The University of Alabama Press
Tuscaloosa

The University of Alabama Press
Tuscaloosa, Alabama 35487-0380
uapress.ua.edu

Manufactured in the United States of America
Book and cover design: Steve Miller
Cover photo: Néstor Martí

Original Spanish-language edition of *Otras cartas a Milena*
published by Ediciones UNIÓN in Havana, 2003.

Permission to use English translations of the two
Anna Akhmatova poems is gratefully acknowledged as follows:
Anna Akhmatova, "The Gray-Eyed King," and "I am not with those who
abandoned their land..." from *Complete Poems of Anna Akhmatova*, translated
by Judith Hemschemeyer, edited and introduced by Roberta Reeder.
Copyright © 1989, 1992, 1997 by Judith Hemschemeyer. Reprinted
with the permission of The Permissions Company, Inc.,
on behalf of Zephyr Press, www.zephyrpress.org.

The paper on which this book is printed meets the minimum requirements
of American National Standard for Information Sciences—Permanence
of Paper for Printed Library Materials, ANSI Z39.48-1984.

Cataloging-in-Publication data is available from the Library of Congress.
ISBN 978-0-8173-5801-3 (paper) — ISBN 978-0-8173-8803-4 (ebook)
ISBN 978-0-8173-9011-2 (deluxe paper edition)

Contents

Acknowledgments

As translator and scholar, I would like to thank the many people who helped to bring my English-language rendition of *Otra cartas a Milena* into existence, often inspiring questions that shaped my introduction to the book. Reina María Rodríguez was tremendously helpful: while discussing this book with me, she took the time to share family photographs as well as personal memories informing the writing, crystallizing images for me as we worked. I would also like to thank her daughter, Elis, for her support for the project; and more specifically, for her patience with potentially invasive questions and practical issues, which arose in a Havana conversation at a time when she was going through major transitions of her own. A cluster of other people contributed to my progress on the book in ways that I (and often they) could not anticipate. Juliet Lynd and Daniel Borzutzky read selected translations with care and offered terrific observations. All errors are of course my own responsibility. Artist Lili Maya, who took some of the texts as a source of ideas for a series of drawings, was an important interlocutor in the early stages of my reflection on the book's contents, which helped me to define the eventual direction of the essay. An invitation from the Americas Society to read with Rodríguez in New York in May 2011 allowed me to take inspiration from the event and its other participants. It also gave me an opportunity to make an audio recording of Rodríguez reading excerpts from this book, now published online by *Asymptote* and linked to the University of Pennsylvania's digital PennSound archive. For their contributions to making the New York event possible, I would like thank Daniel Shapiro and the staff of the Americas Society, who dedicated tremendous energy to the practical challenges involved; as well as Julio Ortega, Jacqueline Loss, Anke Birkenmaier, José Manuel Prieto, and Brian Collier, who facilitated different aspects of the publication, readings, and stay in New York. Joel Kuszai's work with Reina and me during our visit to Queensborough College in 2010 opened up important experiences and conversations about the book, as described in my commentary. Henry Israeli also organized a reading at which I unexpectedly learned more about contexts for this book. Roberto Tejada, Francisco Morán, Charles Hatfield, Rainer Schulte, and Susan Briante supported our visit to Dallas in 2013, which created more valuable opportunities to discuss the manuscript as I prepared it for production. The editors of *Connecticut Review*, *Asymptote*, and *Diálogo* gave encouragement to the book project by publishing excerpts from it. Excerpts also

appeared in *Mandorla: Nueva escritura de las Américas / New Writing from the Americas*. Lastly, I would like to thank the University of Alabama Press and its anonymous reviewers for their thoughtful responses to the manuscript. During our 2013 visit to the Press, Jon Berry's inquiry drew out the importance of Maurice Blanchot's *The Writing of the Disaster* for Rodríguez—a vein of discussion that defies limitation.

Kristin Dykstra

Locating Milena

There's hardly any time left to write to the real Milena,
since the even more real one was here the whole day,
in the room, on the balcony, in the clouds.
Franz Kafka, 29 May 1920

Reina María Rodríguez lives on Ánimas Street, near the corner with San Nicolás, in the city of Havana. An internationally famous poet who won the prestigious Casa de las Américas prize twice in the twentieth century, she has gone on to produce a stream of new works in the twenty-first century. Among her many recent awards is an Italo Calvino prize for her first effort at a novel. In addition to poetry and fiction, Rodríguez has composed poetic prose and essays. The ongoing impact of her career was celebrated in 2013 and 2014 with major national and international recognitions. Rodríguez received Cuba's National Prize for Literature, an event soon followed by the announcement that she had won the Pablo Neruda Ibero-American Prize for Poetry, awarded by Chile's Ministry of Culture.

To date very little of her prose has been translated into English, and none of it appears within the context of a complete book. This translation of her mixed-genre collection *Otras cartas a Milena*, or *Other Letters to Milena*, allows readers to see a more expansive field of her prose, even as that prose appears in tandem with poetry.

First published in Cuba in 2003, *Other Letters to Milena* evokes everyday, remembered, and imagined places around the city. In "A House on Ánimas," for example, Rodríguez brings her poetic ruminations to bear on the street where she has lived for decades. Her richly synthesized language is reminiscent of Virginia Woolf, Anna Akhmatova, and other predecessors forming Rodríguez's pantheon of great writers. As a result this rendition of Ánimas Street is charged with memories, while the writer herself may disappear into oblivion. Such twists complicate Rodríguez's portrait of home, one of many cues alerting readers that the book blends observation and documentation of Havana with other literary modes. Rodríguez explores not only presence but also absence and the richness of the sorrow that shades their coexistence.

The book's title refers to *Letters to Milena*, a collection of letters sent by Franz Kafka to Milena Jesenská, unsettling the portrait of Cuban places with its highly visible gesture of reaching beyond the island, and even beyond the hemisphere, to Eastern Europe. Scholars of Cuban liter-

ature might not be surprised by this move, since they have long asserted the island's complex cultural geographies. For hundreds of years, life and literature in the bustling city of Havana have taken shape in relation to cultural crossings and minglings with the world outside the island's physical shores: "In consequence of its strategic location, the island became a site of convergences, a place of migratory interactions, a circuit and receptacle for all manner of exchanges. . . . Cuban culture is stratified and striated by multiple and varied influences" (O'Reilly Herrera 2). The title *Other Letters to Milena* signals up front that Rodríguez's book will participate in her city's long cosmopolitan tradition.

As I worked through the translation of the book, I began to see that this general observation was not sufficient for understanding the complexity of place in this book or the layering of its title. A more specific issue was emerging: the book's refracted perspectives on the concept of diaspora.

Critical of all of her books in hindsight, Rodríguez states that *Other Letters to Milena* adopts allegorical strategies to discuss topics that remained taboo during the years of its composition. It's an approach that she describes as common in contemporary Cuban literature, and she wonders whether the quality of island writing suffers from so much indirection. In the case of this book, she now describes her refuge in symbolism as an actual flaw in composition. Having worked with Rodríguez on several other projects already, I've often discovered that the features that Rodríguez describes as flaws in her work are the same ones that many readers find to be powerful. A so-called flaw allows the viewer to perceive beauty all around it; a flaw creates greater texture and meaning in the book as a whole. If the gaps and rabbit holes comprising *Other Letters to Milena* compromise any facade of unity or perfection, they also reveal its powerful affinities with other texts, which trump any need for a closed, internal unity of form and content. For example, readers may note its kinship with a work emphasizing the power of the fragment: Maurice Blanchot's *The Writing of the Disaster* (*L'Escriture du désastre*, 1980). Rodríguez remembers the impact of Blanchot's book, which insists on an incremental, patient confrontation with human limitation, incapacity, and disarray. Throughout this introduction I pause to acknowledge similar appearances by other works illustrating the dialogic nature of *Other Letters to Milena*, although my central topic remains the pressing matter of diaspora.

Whether literal or metaphorical, the concept of diaspora relies on an imagined starting point as well as various points of arrival. Rodríguez grounds her diaspora in *Other Letters to Milena* in Havana by tapping into

specific details of island life in the twentieth and early twenty-first centuries. The years 1959 and 1989 mark turning points in Cuban culture, so their legacies are embedded in her scenes. *Other Letters to Milena* then constitutes a meditation on those legacies. It takes up established ways of thinking about home and nation, moving on to rework languages of exile, thus participating in the island's post-1989 turn toward a more flexible concept of diaspora.

Here I trace signs of that shift in cultural vocabularies, which I encountered piece by piece throughout the translation process. Rodríguez creates an embodied response to the transformations of the late twentieth century and the likelihood of further change in the twenty-first. In her hands, exile and diaspora come to encompass social crisis, issues in artistic expression, and subjective experiences of loss. After writing through the literal and metaphorical diasporas of this contemporary period, Rodríguez concludes her book with essays that allow her to reach back into the Cuban literary past—with its own fraught traditions of travel and poetic production—as well as toward other regions in world literature.

As I was finishing my translation, I encountered yet another layer of diasporic experience relevant to the book. I discovered that my choice to translate this book about migration at a particular moment in time hit rather too close to home for Rodríguez, whose family was undergoing great change. At the end of this commentary, I´ll remark on how that situation, awkward as it could have become, makes this book all the more relevant for readers whose own families have undertaken the challenges of migration in the contemporary "age of globalization."

Implicit Contrasts

Through subtle cues from Rodríguez, readers can trace the presence of a persistent opposition in the prose and poetry of *Other Letters to Milena*. The starting point is a mental contrast between life lived "here" on the island and life lived "there" outside. It illustrates a pattern established after 1959 in Cuban discourse, particularly regarding representations of Havana. Velia Cecilia Bobes writes:

> Just as in other cities, self-representation endures some natural disaster (the earthquake of 1985 in Mexico City), some fatal accident (the Great Chicago Fire), or the implantation of urban models (Haussman in Paris)—for Havana, the parting of the waters occurred with the revolution in 1959. This moment defines a before and after in Havana. (16–17)

In the political discourse established in the wake of the Revolution, the

departure of middle and upper class Cubans from the urban capitol for life in exile contributed to the development of a major contrast informing imagined geographies of identity, one that becomes central to *Other Letters to Milena*:

> For Havana the emigration of a good part of its former inhabitants . . . signified the beginning of a relationship with its "mirror city," Miami, where, ninety miles from the coast, those who left began to re-create and re-found the "lost city." With that—and in a context of isolation, the end of tourism, prohibitions on temporarily leaving the country, and so on—imaginary relationships with the exterior are radically changed. (Bobes 20)

The movements of island citizens into exile were associated with fraught political opposition, and over the decades that followed, the tendency to compare Miami and Havana while evoking all manner of other oppositions persisted. Rodriguez specified in our June 2010 conversations about *Other Letters to Milena* that she invokes these historical comparisons and contrasts in subtle ways. After decades of opposition and migration, militancy and mingling, hope and love and disagreements, the contrast between north and south has become so entrenched in her city that Rodríguez only needed to refer to it indirectly. In other words, this is not the element of the book that I am indicating as taboo. Instead it presents an issue of oversaturation, something too common to repeat for initiated audiences. If she laid out her references to this Miami/Havana divide in a more explicit fashion for local readers, her language would seem too crude to produce the ethereal effects that have long characterized her writings. For readers of the translation who live elsewhere, though, I emphasize this context to reveal how she has made her writing complex: not by distancing herself from her society and history, as less initiated readers sometimes assume at first glance due to the subtlety of her cues, but by subjecting the everyday to unusually intense aesthetic exploration.

Rodríguez's study of life in Havana registers life in a home overlooking Ánimas (the "street of souls," where her apartment building is located a few blocks away from the ocean) in relation to her strong awareness of past and present migrations across the ninety miles separating the island from the United States. The Havana vs. Miami contrast of the exilic mode persists in the language and imagery of *Other Letters to Milena*. In her portrait of life along Ánimas, for example, Rodríguez pauses to dwell on goods sent from "Mayami" for a wedding. It is a quick but effective illustration of how, during the island's first intensifying economic crisis of the post-Soviet moment, "the mirror relationship with Miami is inten-

sified and repaired with the increased flexibility of the migratory policy that fosters the visits and economic aid of emigrants to their families" (Bobes 27). This aid exists despite the ongoing United States embargo of Cuba, a potent symbol of the extended political opposition marking international relations for decades. In other pieces from *Other Letters to Milena*, such as "The Girl's Story," the exilic opposition is still there but not surfaced in such explicit ways: for example, Rodríguez discussed with me the fact that her semi-coded phrases about "the other shore" refer to the Floridian side of that mirror.

In the late twentieth century, a preliminary variation on imagery of exile appeared in Cuba: an inversion of exile that is applied to experiences of life on the island itself. *Insilio*, or the exile within, is a general term that has been used in criticism about works from Cuba and other nations in Latin America where exile has been a significant phenomenon (such as Chile and Uruguay). The physical imprisonment of gay writer Reinaldo Arenas (1943–1990), for example, accompanied his social and political castigation while he was living in Cuba. This resulted in his depiction of a sensation of exile from society in his major works propelled by experiences of alienation and oppression (Gutiérrez). *Insilio* can also refer to works expressing a sort of social death in life, an interior entrapment that need not involve the literal imprisonment suffered by Arenas. With this broader definition in mind, *Other Letters to Milena* can arguably be read as a work of insilio. However, this approach stills need to take up other context from the book's time period, including discussion of diasporic discourse.

As she channels the entrenched imagery of opposition surrounding exile, Rodríguez simultaneously engages a new turn from post-1989 Cuba: a gradual shift toward reimagining displacement in terms of diaspora. The locations and meanings of outsiderness expand over the course of her book, often leaving southern Florida and the post-1959 northern exile behind, to acknowledge other locations and connotations. To my mind the coexistence of these two vocabularies, sets of terms and ideas clustered around exile and diaspora, yield the most complex aspects of the book's socio-historical content. There is no way to fully detach the two models from each other.

Rodríguez does not depict migrations from the migrant's perspective, a topic explored elsewhere by writers who have themselves moved into new lives abroad. She offers the perspective of someone who attempts to stay and inhabit the capital city, albeit with periodic short visits to other places. Whether we refer to exile or diaspora, hers is the face of the figure left behind, the writer who hopes to reconstruct a world poten-

tially still vibrant, still growing and changing, even when it is increasingly populated by the ghosts of people once present on her daily walks. Ruth Behar observed in 2008 that the figure who remains behind had become a familiar one in Cuban society due to the intensity of resettlement:

> Back on the island, it is the responsibility of those who stay to wave goodbye and shed tears for the departed. . . . Movements back and forth, from the island to the diaspora, or from the diaspora to the island, between cities, between continents, and across oceans and rivers have made travelers of us all, even Cubans who only dream of going places. (3)

Other Letters to Milena then expresses ways in which migration in the contemporary moment reconfigures cities and islands of origin, not just the people who travel and their destinations.

Another element of the gaze brought by Rodríguez to this topic is the perspective of a parent concerned about the world taking shape for her children. The mapping of Cuban life took new turns after 1989 with the onset of economic crisis and the uncertain prospects of the post–Cold-War world. More than ever, staying put in Havana was a choice that a parent made not only as an individual, but on behalf of a family. The figure of Rodríguez's daughter, Elis Milena, haunts this book. The youngest of the author's four children, Elis was still quite small as the Special Period took hold. Rodríguez explicitly writes about the experience raising a child amid crisis in "The Girl's Story," a series addressed to Elis. The epistolary style of several pieces in the series makes the daughter's presence palpable. The book's title therefore shelters the daughter, naming her at the same time it names Kafka's literary interlocutor, Milena Jesenská.

Through Elis the book raises questions for the next generation. Will the daughter grow up to be another ghost, floating across the distances of diaspora? Or will she still walk through her mother's city shadowing the same routes they once followed together?

A Poetics of Recalibration

Statements like "we play at escaping ruination for a second," found in one of the texts depicting mother and daughter in "The Girl's Story," reveal an immediate source for the sadness and disorientation, a sort of home-lessness, permeating this book. The writer struggles to draw her characteristically ethereal, suggestive poetic beauty out of a harsh new scene of economic disaster, and she cannot seem to figure out how one would make art without inadvertently taking advantage of the community's pain.

"The Girl's Story" shares insights as to how disaster becomes psychological and even aesthetic.

Rodríguez began writing many of these texts in the mid-1990s, as Cubans scrambled to respond to the increasing severity of crisis. Because "the post-Soviet present continues to be a time of dramatic change and intense uncertainty" in Havana in the new century, the issues she raised during the composition of her book continue to weigh upon residents of the city and visitors alike (Birkenmaier 4).

More specifically, *Other Letters to Milena* displays many traces of the moment known euphemistically as Cuba's "Special Period." Global political realignments of the late twentieth century had led to the loss of the island's established allies and trade partners in the Soviet Union, setting off a sharp series of transitions into a post-Soviet economy. Difficulties accessing essential supplies, such as petroleum and food, translated into pressing shortages for islanders in the 1990s. Meanwhile the ongoing US trade embargo continued to restrict options for restructuring the economy. Among other coping strategies, island leaders found themselves forced to resuscitate the tourist economy, a force they had sought to restrain in earlier decades. Increasingly desperate individuals undertook economic migration, while others sought survival through black market activity and prostitution. Paper shortages constricted professional opportunities for writers, both at the composition stage and that of publication; and the Eastern European market for their work dried up (Buckwalter-Arias 363).

Buildings in Havana became famous for their symbolic degradation due to a lack of resources for repair and renovation. Their highly visible ruination rapidly became a common metaphor for writers, artists, and filmmakers. "What Havana is, or what it is becoming, is open to question for its inhabitants and viewers," observe Anke Birkenmaier and Esther Whitfield, noting that the island's many visitors often interpret this landscape in a particular way: they have assumed that "architectural decay signaled the inevitable decline of Cuba's socialist project" (4). Yet Havana's future remains a subject of intense, unresolved debate. For many scholars, this is an important point to emphasize because the media is full of proclamations about the island's future, as well as unstated but influential assumptions. We cannot presume to know that the island is moving down a neatly laid train track toward an inevitable future that we can name; it's necessary to admit a lack of knowledge, a gap in understanding, even if we want to guess at the island's future or, as in the case of writers and artists, begin to construct a new vision for Cuban society.

Dwelling in a neighborhood with its own ruins, inside a rooftop home built by hand from recycled parts, with a mesmerizing view across the changing city and its border at the sea, Rodríguez dug into the experience of existing in Havana amid the crisis. She suggested in a recent interview that her literary treatment of Havana's ruins differs from the use fellow writers have made of them: rather than adopting the external gaze of a pedestrian contemplating buildings (as have many photographers), or the structured vision of a fiction writer who uses ruins as architecture giving form to a narrated world, she uses poetry and poetic prose to "consume" her surroundings ("Como de camino hacia un parque,"). In *Other Letters to Milena*, the speaker's existence parallels that of the city, spreads into it, infiltrates its spaces—and in a surprising turn, insists that the city can be taken inside the self. As an artistic strategy, this might be seen as a mode of relation that allows the artist to envision a modicum of control over her environment: a way to imagine breaking the city down into basic resources, prior to creating something new out of its parts.

Rodríguez's references to Samuel Beckett, deployed in "The Girl's Story" to describe her artistic community in crisis, evoke her search for new ways of consuming and generating ruination through writing. She specifically names Beckett's "Lessness," a work of short fiction which begins with this sentence: "Ruins true refuge long last towards which so many false time out of mind" (197). It is a chain whose meanings can be dismantled and rearticulated as the reader focuses on its constituent word-parts. Although Beckett warns us within that quotation that the progress embodied in the words "towards which" may turn out to be a repetitive falsehood, an anonymous figure still struggles to progress through the scene in the story as a whole: "One step in the ruins in the sand on his back in the endlessness he will make it. . . . Face to white calm touch close eye calm long last all gone from mind. One step more one alone all alone in the sand no hold he will make it" (198). Another Beckett piece that Rodríguez cites, "The Lost Ones," also presents an abstract, impossible quest: "Abode where lost bodies roam each searching for its lost one. Vast enough for search to be in vain. Narrow enough for flight to be in vain" (202). Battling to ascend a ladder missing half its rungs— apparently the only trajectory available to them—his lost bodies do violence to each other. Fragments of Beckett's texts reappear throughout "The Girl's Story," suggesting that Beckett himself has been consumed, converted into shards of warning and figure by Rodríguez.

Just as Beckett challenged progress narratives with his treatment of ruination, so too did Cuban poets in the new century. Previously favored progress narratives about the island's leading role in world history,

like the seemingly solid walls of its buildings, were giving way. The nation itself seemed to become other: "In the Special Period, there was a 'before,' which was stable, perhaps purer in its altruism and high ideals, a 'now,' which was confusing and unsettling, and a future that was, for many, another country" (Hernández-Reguant 2). The next stage for writers, presumably, would be the crafting of a new and different narrative or set of images. For poets like Rodríguez, a new equilibrium had to be sought for writing, a new aesthetic, at a moment when generating it might prove impossible. Breaking down the scene and reconsidering its parts would be more than an aesthetic move; it would become a necessary confrontation with overwhelming, unclear spatial and temporal modes.

For others, the key strategy would be physical departure: the trajectory of diaspora.

1994

Paired with imagery of oceans, rafts, and migration, occasional dates appear in *Other Letters to Milena*. They call a specific type of migration to mind, one that serves as a metaphor for extreme disruptions of balance in contemporary Cuban life. While I worked through the translation of the book, an awareness of this context heightened my sense of its dynamism: that is, the weave Rodríguez creates out of diverse registers of meaning.

María Cristina García has charted major waves of Cuban migration in the late twentieth century in a well-known study with a timeline ending circa 1994, *Havana USA*. In García's formulation, the first three major waves of post-1959 movement from the island to the United States occurred in the immediate post-revolution years of 1959–1962, the "Freedom Flight" years of 1965–1973, and the Mariel Boatlift events of 1980. Each group of Cuban migrants differed from the others in many ways; García succeeds in showing that migration is a complex and ever-changing phenomenon, affecting the way Cubans have understood their lives in both the island and exile, which increasingly reimagines itself as diaspora. A fourth peak in migration is represented by 1994, a date Rodríguez places on several texts in *Other Letters to Milena*.

This year is associated with the *balseros*, or rafters, who set out in homemade rafts and small boats to cross the Florida Straits. García writes, "The balseros of 1994 are different [from the earlier three migrant groups] in the sheer number of people who have made the journey. In one five-week period alone, from August 5 to September 10, the US Coast Guard picked up 30,305 Cubans at sea. These balseros are also different in that they left their homeland with tacit approval from the Castro government" (ix). Many individuals did not survive the voyage, a fact that heightens the

tension of Rodríguez's compact set of four prose poems near the beginning of *Other Letters to Milena*: "Passage of Clouds," "The Octopus," "The Figurehead," and "The Photographer."

As I've previously noted, imagery of exile had long focused on the Havana/Miami pairing. However, Behar explains that with the turn into the twenty-first century, Cubans "also resettled permanently in a wider range of cities in Europe and Latin America. Even in the United States, while Miami remains the classical Cuban hub, it is no longer the primary destination for the newest wave of Cuban immigrant writers and intellectuals" (7). Expanding on this description of a changing map, Hernández-Reguant has demonstrated that a "redefinition of the Cuban nation as an ethnic and cultural community," rather than a specific political community, had been gradually taking place over the course of the 1990s (72). A major outcome of this redefinition "was the disentanglement of nation from territory; effectively, the incorporation into the nation of the much vilified exile community now refashioned as a 'diaspora,'" a word more acceptable to island authorities (72). One motivation for accepting this redefinition of exile was financial; the relaxation of political stances could make it easier to bring in support from the Cuban community in the US, as various scholars have observed. Important as that financial motive would be in a context of economic crisis, it is not the only factor to note. The term "diaspora" was flexible enough to account for Cubans who had left the island to live elsewhere (not always in the US) while still retaining an open relationship to their nation, rather than pointing toward the specific political oppositionality connoted by language about post-1959 exile. It also accompanied increasing openness to other conceptualizations of diversity. "The notion of a transnational or hybrid identity presents an interesting personal and political vision for diaspora communities," observes political scientist María de los Angeles Torres. "It proposes not only that communities be transformed, but that their host and home countries undergo transformation as well" (381–382).

Changes in the perception of "Cubanness" across territorial and/or national borders were therefore part of a large-scale, post-Soviet remapping of ideologies:

> As frontiers were being undone in Eastern Europe, and the European Union extended its domain considerably, in Cuba the limits of *cubanía* were being rethought and the idea of a common culture of "Greater Cuba," with hubs not only in Havana and Miami but also in other European, Latin American, and US cities, was being articulated. (Birkenmaier 6)

As this shift percolated through island society, academic institutions began supporting projects in various disciplines that emphasized a widening framework of nationhood in relation to culture. By the mid-1990s, artists and writers on the island were carrying out active remappings to their fields of reference. Tania Bruguera's alternative art space El Espacio Aglutinador was showing art produced both abroad and in marginalized island circumstances; meanwhile, leaders of the literary review *Diaspora(s)*, who also carried out their project in an unofficial manner, similarly sought to deterritorialize national literature (Hernández-Reguant 78). The Havana Biennials began to become sites of international exchange among Cubans living in different places (Birkenmaier 6). These changes did not fully unmake the political oppositions still attached to lived realities, and therefore the discourse of diaspora has not fully overthrown the structures of exile, but the shift had a meaningful impact nonetheless.

That impact is seen here, in the world of post-1989 literature. In the texts that eventually became *Other Letters to Milena*, Rodríguez was taking up the term *diaspora*, pushing at its boundaries, refashioning it. In keeping with her frequent use of ambivalence in poetry, she would work back and forth between Havana's public discourse and her own defamiliarizing twists in her new project.

Another Exile

> *I confess to a friend . . . that I don't want to write a chronicle of reality but a chronicle of irreality. However, the term is very hard for me to define. I realize that the only word I have to describe it is precisely that: irreality. I reiterate to my friend: I don't want to discover how Cubans (more specifically, habaneros) really live; I prefer to think about the different ways they imagine themselves living.*
> José Quiroga
> "Bitter Daiquiris" 275

Diaspora took on both lived and imaginary facets for Rodríguez. Distances from the departed and the lost cast shadows across the faces of people who did not get on the rafts or airplanes. In *Other Letters to Milena*, the people who stay behind don't speak in order to pass judgment on migrants but to delineate a situation. Its degrees of distance from those who are going or gone generate a kind of exile experienced by the person who has not moved but whose anchors have shifted: colleagues, dear friends, loved ones.

As an internationally recognized writer, Rodríguez has periodic opportunities for short professional travels in other countries, and these trips have been extremely important for her for personal and creative reasons. Many people once central for her personal and artistic life now live in Europe, in the United States, or elsewhere in Latin America; on her trips she gets to reunite briefly with some of them. Some return for short visits to the island. Yet she has regularly referred to the impact of their absence from the theater of everyday life in Havana. The loss of many writers important to her as part of a professional support system represents a significant absence, one to which she has referred many times in our past conversations. Other losses include people with whom she had more intimate relationships, setting up a specific twist to ruminations on romance, hope, and the passage of time in her writing.

In our conversations about *Other Letters to Milena*, Rodríguez told me that for many years overlapping with its composition she held onto the illusion that by refusing to leave Havana, she could somehow hold up its buildings with the force of her mind. If she just looked at objects one day after another, she imagined, she could stave off their loss. As a corollary to this vision she began to feel guilty about traveling, even when she received professional invitations and the requisite governmental permission to take short trips abroad. These feelings became so convincing that she once broke down after boarding a plane and got off before takeoff, a moment she incorporated into "The Girl´s Story."

Travel is relevant both in the pages of this book and in her life as a writer in general. A different sort of impediment to travel affecting Cubans in general in recent decades, preventing some reunions and stifling relationships, is that official permissions are not always given by one government or another in the US/Cuban standoff. This reminder of earlier decades of opposition kept Rodríguez from making the crossing from Havana to the United States from 2001 to 2009 to accept professional invitations, to her disappointment, although she was permitted to enter the United States more recently.

Writers, Divided: The Original Letters to Milena

Given the context of a community fractured into many distances, it's not hard to see why Rodríguez would take an interest in the letters exchanged between two literary lovers whose writing was occasioned by their separation: Franz Kafka and the Czech journalist and translator Milena Jesenská (1896–1944). Some of their letters—only his letters, written to her, and

carefully preserved—were published after their deaths under the title *Letters to Milena*, causing a splash in the literary world of 1952. Jesenská's surname never appeared in that collection, and her half of their correspondence is exiled to nowhere.

Jesenská was the only writer among the women Kafka loved, so the loss of her letters contributes to the ghostly qualities of his surviving texts. Rodríguez has composed other works in response to literary women—their work, their lives and images—and clearly takes an interest in Jesenská on multiple levels. Jesenská becomes a touchstone for meditations on literature, aging, death, relationships, and distance. Here I'll briefly trace details that helped me to understand her fragmented appearances in this book as I was working through the translation.

Jesenská and Kafka wrote their letters back and forth across the distances between Prague and Vienna. Milena Jesenská had become an active member of cultural circles in Prague following World War I. There she crossed the de facto boundaries separating the circles of the Czech intelligentsia from those of the German Jews, much to her father's distaste. Each circle had "its own publishing houses, magazines, newspapers, coffeehouses," observes George Gibian, and "very few Czechs bridged the gap; Milena was one of those few" (4). In 1918 Jesenská married Ernst Polak, a prominent member of the German scene in Prague whom she had met through work on an anthology of Czech poetry. Jesenská and Polak moved together to Vienna. There the couple soon appeared in coffeehouses where they met intellectuals interested in the activity back in Prague. Jesenská began to write *feuilletons* (a genre related to the personal essay) describing Viennese culture for publications in Prague, and she translated samples of its literature. On a return visit to Prague in October 1919, Jesenská met Franz Kafka in a coffeehouse. Once back in Vienna, she contacted him with an offer to translate some of his work into Czech. He consented, and their correspondence commenced. Jesenská completed a chapter from his novel *Amerika*, which was published in April 1920 in a Czech literary weekly. The correspondence that had begun as a professional exchange soon became more personal and intimate. Both writers were involved with other people. However, Jesenská and Polak were having marital problems. In her letters to Kafka Jesenská apparently described her husband's affairs with other women, her loneliness, and more. Kafka, who had begun to write letters to Jesenská more and more frequently, eventually offered to help Jesenská leave her husband; she declined his help.

Their correspondence retained its vivid intellectual nature, one

of its most striking qualities. Each writer was simultaneously absent and present to the interlocutor on the other end of the letter. After it became clear that their relationship had intensified into a blend of intellect and romance, they crossed that gap to meet in person for four days in late June and early July, when Kafka visited Vienna. The letters record intimacy, love, and desire as well as intellectual sharing. But the relationship failed to further materialize in person, reverting to a written state.

Most correspondence between the two writers took place through January 1921, with a few final exchanges up to 1923. Although Jesenská's letters are lost, other writings remain, notably an obituary she composed upon Kafka´s death. She portrayed Kafka's death as an inability to live, gesturing beyond his literal illness to a quality she perceived in his literature and general psychology. Kafka's letters, in turn, caused a splash that made Jesenská famous—as "his" Milena—after her death. They held biographical interest as documents that revealed more reflection from the writer about himself, as a person, than other sources.

Relations Found and Lost

Of what did this relationship between Kafka and Jesenská most truly exist? Translator Philip Boehm writes, "The letters themselves do not merely reflect the stages of the relationship, they *are* the relationship" (xv). Rodríguez, who considers the same question in *Other Letters to Milena*, ultimately decides that she doesn't know. Perhaps it is the ghostly presence of the other, the terror of a more physical encounter that matters. Or their relationship is really "about" Kafka's halting speech about failure in relationships and his fear of failing again—about the gaps in his attempts to explain his need for distance:

> I don't want (Milena, help me! Understand more than I am saying) I don't want (this isn't stuttering) to come to Vienna, because I couldn't stand the mental stress. I am spiritually ill, my lung disease is nothing but an overflowing of my spiritual disease. . . . I can't write anything more, explain anything more; of course I should mention the other reasons for not leaving. (31 May 1920)

It may be irrelevant to trace the life of Milena, understood as Jesenská the historical person, for the remainder of this commentary: it is "Kafka's Milena," created on paper, who has been so influential.

Still, this pattern may be more complex with Rodríguez. She has displayed a significant pattern of fascination with women writers: her ghostly Jesenská falls into a line including Sylvia Plath, Virginia Woolf, Marina

Tsvetaeva, and many others whom she has transformed into images, provocations for her own writing.[1] The image of Milena has allowed Rodríguez to explore metaphorical dimensions of experience more than anything else, but there are some suggestively literal elements of Jesenská here, in addition to the distances between writers that I've highlighted already. If in Kafka's letters Milena is the absent beloved addressed by a writer, the real Jesenská never did settle into a stable, lasting marriage to Kafka or anyone else. For Rodríguez the theme of failed romantic partnerships repeats across many books. Variations on the topic, such as distrust of marriage as an institution and frustration at the collapse of long-term relationships, appear in *Catch and Release* (from Editorial Letras Cubanas, 2006) and *Las fotos de la Señora Loss* (*Photos from Mrs. Loss*, published by the Spanish Embassy in Cuba, 2009), to name only two of her more recent titles. Jesenská's poor relationship with another symbolic male figure, her father, also left a mark on her life and work, making Rodríguez's "Bishops" a fitting addition to this collection, with its exploration of distances from her own father.

And what of the fate of the real Milena? Jesenská was interned at the Ravensbruck concentration camp. There she became a close friend to her fellow prisoner Margarete Buber-Neumann. Jesenská died at Ravensbruck, but Buber-Neumann survived to tell her tale, publishing a book about her friend in 1963 entitled *Kafkas Freundin Milena*. Thus Milena returns from the camp in Rodríguez's book "with the sulfurous odor of crematories still on her skin" ("The Girl's Story," V).

The Short Essays

> *The future does not exist. It does not lie in store*
> *and does not await us. It is prescribed by no one.*
> Nina Berberova, *The Italics Are Mine*, 30

The essays comprising the final section of *Other Letters to Milena* revisit diaspora in their own ways. Some expand on a relationship to Eastern Europe and the Soviet Union. This suggests a lingering awareness of a "post-Soviet life" in Cuba's Special Period. Reversing the possibility that Russia will merely disappear from the Cuban field of attention at the dawn of the twenty-first century, Rodríguez reasserts the presences of Brodsky, Akhmatova, Tsvetaeva, Berberova, Blok, and others in the cultural panorama of her book.

[1] For English-language readers, the collections *La detención del tiempo* / *Time's Arrest* and *Violet Island and Other Poems* contain additional examples of this kind of intertextuality. See also note 4.

Jacqueline Loss has suggested that contemporary culture evoking the presence of the Soviet Union in Cuban life and memory may raise questions about the island's presumed future, particularly "the degree to which we may envision Cuba as involved in a teleological passage toward capitalism" (120). In my discussions of the book with Rodríguez, she confirmed that these essays were motivated by a cluster of factors surrounding Russian writers, some of which meld nicely with Loss's observation. One is her partial identification with the sound of the writers' names and the Russian language: Russian is a foreign language for her, and yet it retains a familiar feel, because her own brother spoke it. The language has not merely been erased from history or her present writings in the post-Soviet moment. Rodríguez was also taken with the fact that these writers had experienced forms of exile. Related to that point, yet not reducible to it, she described them to me as political writers. A series of ideas and images emerge for her out of this "land of tyrants and czars": the role of utopia in the social imagination; questions about how those utopian visions relate to the passage of historical time; the region's transition from feudalism to today´s system; and an uncertainty about how, precisely, to classify the post-Soviet societies existing in that part of the world today. In this same reflection, Rodríguez referred to her interest in the image of a Russian soul that remains "incumplido," unrealized or unfulfilled (email from 6 June 2011).

Readers interested in these interpretive possibilities for the essays must consider how they are embodied in her imagery and citation. Rather than overt sociopolitical commentary, a series of relationships with the dead dominate the essays as a group. An interplay between liberty and constraint links Rodríguez's essays to other texts in this collection, as does the opposition between presence and absence. Her speakers are there and not there, occupying spaces, traversing the distances between them to link the theme of exile to that of mortality. Overall the short essays she included in *Other Letters to Milena* reveal more about Rodríguez and her writing—such as significant contexts and her ongoing quest to develop aesthetic angles over the course of years—than the people and literature she describes.

"Bishops" and "The Grave" explore memory, immediate family life, and tragedy. It will be clear to the reader that "Bishops" refers to the death of Rodríguez's father and provides a local context for the chess imagery[2]

---

[2] Bishop is not only the name of a chess piece but also the name of a famous street in Havana (Obispo). When translating I sometimes had to choose usage. If the main goal were to evoke a feel for the streets of Havana, my preference would be to use Obispo—but then the connection to the chess game, and the emotions Rodríguez evokes with it, becomes obscure for readers who can't access both languages.

that reappears in the final short text concluding the book. Somewhat more ambiguous is "The Grave": this essay, Rodríguez specifies, refers to her brother's death, which took place fifteen days before the birth of her son Edgar (who presently lives in Barcelona, adding another layer of lived diasporic context to the existence of this book). Rodríguez found it a powerful enough experience to write these pieces that she returned to "Bishops" in a subsequent book, *Galiano St. Variety*, creating a revised version of this same essay. There she also returned to the figure of Diotima, the cat who lived with her family for years in the apartment overlooking Ánimas Street, crafting a separate piece entitled "Diotima (The second text for her)."[3]

These family essays may at first seem distinct from the reflections on eastern European and Russian writers. A little extra acquaintance with the works Rodríguez cites, however, makes it hard to avoid seeing connections. For example, Nina Berberova's autobiography (cited on page xxx) includes a dream reminiscent of "Bishops." Berberova dreams that she is playing chess while Dostoevsky looks on. Dostoevsky tells Berberova:

> Twenty-five or thirty moves you can, of course, foresee, but only on the condition that the ceiling does not collapse during the game and that one of the players does not die of a stroke. If this happens, then chess becomes like life, it moves into a dimension where there are neither social nor biological laws, nor the possibility for the smartest mind to figure out the 'pattern' of the future (34).

What better description of the sudden death of Rodríguez's chess-playing father, which leads his daughter precisely toward this uncertain mode of existence, evoked through "the color of a certain zone" on the mind?

"A Cemetery for Her," the essay exploring the poetry of Anna Akhmatova, concludes in the original Cuban edition with reprints of two poems by the Russian writer on the topic of making a choice: whether to stay in one's community or depart. The terms for diaspora and *destierro*, a word for exile used in Cuban traditions past and present, bleed into Akhmatova's world. This opening, a triangulation, prevents the literary exploration of diaspora from stagnating in the familiar post-1959 binary opposition between Havana and Miami.

Readers familiar with Rodríguez's larger body of writing will also recognize that she has translated details from the essays on these Russian

[3] English translation forthcoming in *The Havana Reader*, published by Duke University Press, ed. José Quiroga and Francisco Morán.

writers into her poems from recent decades. For example, "The Devil" will initially look like a review Rodríguez composed about a newly released book of translated Russian literature, and up to a point it is. Yet readers who have spent time with her other books will notice that they've seen references to Marina Tsvetaeva and much of this same imagery before. The essays on Russian writers thus become suggestive companion texts to her other creative writing, revealing ways in which Rodríguez pushed herself to create new work through a process of drawing on international sources.[4]

The essay on Heberto Padilla's death, which ended his campaign for permission to visit the island from which he had been exiled, is likely to draw attention for merging an especially controversial figure into this theater populated by literary Russians. Padilla left Cuba many decades ago amid internationally famous conflicts with the island's cultural institutions. Padilla's case involved a series of events usually said to have been kicked off by two literary incidents: his 1968 UNEAC award for a poetry collection of which authorities did not approve, followed by retroactive criticism of his 1967 show of support for writer Guillermo Cabrera Infante, who had fallen out of favor with the government and left the country. Subsequent incidents included but were not limited to Padilla's 1971 detention, a forced public "confession" in which he recanted and denounced fellow intellectuals, and his eventual departure from Cuba in 1980.

The following excerpt concludes a poem in Padilla's famous collection *Fuera del juego* (*Sent Out of the Game*). Jorge Guitart's translation, "In Hard Times," was first published in the United States in 1973:

They asked him for the woods
that nourished him as a child
with its obedient trees.
They asked him for his chest, his heart, his shoulders.
They told him that it was strictly necessary.
They explained to him later
that all these donations would be useless
unless he also surrender his tongue
because during hard times
nothing could be more useful
for stopping hatred or lies.

---

[4] Two examples available in English translation: A piece called "The Devil" appears in English translation in *La detención del tiempo / Time's Arrest*, Factory School, 2nd ed., 2005; a poem drawing on the imagery of blood, "The Mother, The Piano," names "Marina" and appears in *Bombay Gin* 37.1: 146–149.

And finally they asked him politely
to start moving
because during hard times
this is, no doubt, the decisive test. (22–36)

Padilla's name has come to be associated not only with the individual ex-
ile of a writer, or poems delivering political observation with dark humor,
but concerns about the state of artistic expression under the Cuban gov-
ernment. His case is seen as "an account of official persecution, domi-
nation, repression and humiliation" (Cortina 54). It sent cracks through
the international left. After word of Padilla's detention got out, European
writers who had previously expressed support for the Castro government
sent an open letter criticizing this turn of events. Among them were Jean-
Paul Sartre, Simone de Beauvoir, Italo Calvino, and Marguerite Duras.
A subsequent letter included Nathalie Sarraute and Susan Sontag. Re-
actions begat reactions, and scholars have linked the incidents involving
Padilla to statements then made by Fidel Castro in 1971 on the subject of
artists, writers, intellectuals, and revolution; and to the famous polemical
essay "Caliban," by Roberto Fernández Retamar, a powerful statement
on language and culture which became a staple in postcolonial studies as
well as sections of US Latino studies (Buckwalter-Arias, Ortiz).

By writing about Padilla and his thwarted desire to return to the
island, then, Rodríguez assumes the risk of losing control over shards
of the powerful, oppositional, refractory public rhetoric she has handled
with care in other parts of this book. If, as Hernández-Reguant has ar-
gued, the Special Period represented an official loosening of policy re-
garding exiles, what was still at stake in public and intellectual circles in
the request of one of its most controversial writers to return? In taking on
the role of an advocate for his return? In mourning that lost opportunity?

A great deal of material has been published on the Padilla affair as
it played out in the 1960s and 1970s. I will not add more to the summary
here: Rodríguez herself does not rehearse those earlier events, a strategy
I find significant to her handling of this topic. Instead she uses her essay
to show how, as a writer living on the island, she could engage a colleague
living on the other side of the divide decades after his departure in spite
of the extensive cultural chain reactions associated with it. In addition to
retaining some familiarity with names and works of the departed—albeit
a familiarity restrained by significant factors, such as a systematic lack of
access to books published abroad—writers in Cuba have become aware of
some colleagues in diaspora in new ways. As she shows here, this is par-
ticularly effective if they have chanced to meet during their travels, which

allow writers to get to know each other as people instead of reputations or (as in Padilla's case) staggering international legacies.[5] Meeting in Stockholm, Rodríguez and Padilla have the advantage of a new setting, where pasts and paranoia lurk but do not determine all interactions. Her essay evokes the complexities of a greater Cuban literary scene, one in which exiled, diasporic, and island writers seek out ways to pursue new conversations across borders rather than endlessly circling around the moment and circumstances in which someone left, or obeying a tired language of opposition. This process arguably allows for an understanding that "the diasporic subject is always in a state of movement and transition—wholly belonging neither here/*aquí*, nor there/*allá*," so that Rodríguez moves on to locate her ultimate site of "spatial" identification with Padilla in the pages of his writing (O'Reilly Herrera 205).

Other Letters to Milena also disrupts potentially suffocating elements of the post-1959 opposition in temporal terms, provoking the reader to reconsider the historical span at stake.[6] The very short essay "The Voice of the Niagara" serves as a recognizable reference to Cuban literary exile, tapping into a multi-canonical source of energy: a famous nineteenth-century poem by José María Heredia. One of the most important Romantic poets of Latin America, Heredia was exiled from the island during the colonial period for his activity promoting independence from Spain. He is one of several prominent figures illustrating the point that Cuban exile in other Americas not only occurred long before 1959 but led to significant literary expression. Writing by nineteenth-century exiles, now seen as important precursors to US Latino literary traditions of exile, has inspired reflection on that term *destierro* which Rodríguez uses in her book. Rodrigo Lazo observes that in the nineteenth-century context many exiles called themselves *desterrados*, or people who are deterritorialized. He adds:

> While a common translation for *desterrado* is exile, the Spanish term has lexical and connotative dimensions that are not captured

[5] See Buckwalter-Arias for important observations about the asymmetrical circulation of literary works in recent decades, a situation in which literature published abroad will often be unimaginably expensive for the average Cuban, even as supply is limited in terms of the number of publications that arrive on the island to be purchased at all. This print culture phenomenon has been aggravated by a low rate of connectivity to the Internet for islanders.

[6] This type of intervention in the historical and geographical span of Cuban diaspora represents an important strategy also employed by writers living outside Cuba at this time. I suggest juxtaposing *Other Letters to Milena* with the novel *Days of Awe* (NY: Ballantine, 2001), by Achy Obejas: Obejas doubles diaspora, complicating post-1959 trajectories of exile and return through their intersections with extended histories of Jewish migration in the Americas. Blending literary observation with cultural criticism, José Quiroga has meddled with time and space all the more by writing in terms of *Cuban Palimpsests* (Minneapolis: University of Minnesota Press, 2005) in which their bounds collapse.

by the English. *Desterrado* emphasizes a tearing away from the land; thus, to be a Cuban *desterrado* destabilizes the association of territory and nation that has marked many of the seminal texts defining Cubanness. (14)

The literary imagery folds place against placelessness: the nineteenth-century exiles expressed a strong desire to be connected to their nation-as-territory even as they documented the sense of being torn away.

Lazo describes this earlier longing as a different model of nationhood than the one adopted by many of today's Cuban exiles, who have developed a more "fluid sense of self and nation" over the course of decades of existing outside the island's physical territory (14). In addition to the shifts in island discourse regarding diaspora in the 1990s that I noted earlier in this essay, understandings of national identity today have also been transformed by globalization, vast migrations among many countries around the world, and the changing interpretations of national space and culture these interconnections entail. Meanwhile, another powerful shift has come with the reinterpretation of individual national cultures in light of multiculturalism: nations are now seen to be far less pure and isolated than previously imagined. Rodríguez, whose work echoes with many of these very contemporary turns, has gone back to the nineteenth century to incorporate Heredia into the scope of her book: why?

One reason may be the very complication Heredia presents to definitions of national culture, the evidence of a historical transnationalism in which exile culminated in literature: that is, exile led to work that is now accepted as canonical culture, while it simultaneously undermines and reinstates the oppositions between "here" and "there." Precursors such as Heredia, though pursuing a different vision of nation, offer important evidence that national literatures in the Americas have always been historically entangled: "To read these as writers solely of Cuba or solely as part of a US tradition is to miss the multiple locations of writings that crossed languages, national borders, and sociocultural contexts" (Lazo 15). Heredia's classic poem about Niagara Falls, a site simultaneously dividing and unifying a pair of nations in the Americas, presents several conventions later repeated in literature about that place. He didn't depict just the Falls themselves but added a memory of Caribbean landscapes, turning his poem into a transnational platform for reflection on exile in the Americas. Alienation from Cuba infuses the poem with extra meanings, including longing for an absent beloved, who parallels the absent physical (and proto-national) island landscape. Kirsten Silva Gruesz explains, "Heredia inaugurates a thematic of eroticized nationalism, of *poesía civil interna*, that anchors a distinct tradition

of Latin American poetry to come" (43). A visit to Niagara Falls continues to be a staple activity for traveling Latin American writers on their visits to the northeastern United States, even if their itinerary wouldn't otherwise take them to that part of the border (Gruesz 31). Rodríguez visited the Falls during a visit to Buffalo in 2000, when she was invited to present her poetry at the State University of New York. Her resulting text evokes the iconic itinerary and so participates—consciously albeit briefly—in the trans-American tradition. She identifies a voice for the water, harking back to Heredia's lines, and asserts the loss of the writer's control over the scene she surveys, a key element of the sublime literary moment.

The brevity of her experiment in this essay on the Falls, however, is a good reminder that she may identify far more with Beckett than Heredia, whose speaker called for a lyre to capture the powerful sensations the Falls created in his bosom. Beckett, observes Gontarski, caricatures Romantic descriptions of "the artist's agonized communion with his own pure, uncorrupted inner being, consciousness, or imagination" (xvii). For Rodríguez, a related and even more contemporary challenge comes from the speed with which history seems to move: she acknowledges the frustrations of hyperrealism, in which her language can never catch up to the world she sees—this produces a deferral of communion with no endpoint in sight. Any comprehension of the speaker's place in time and space remains blurry, deferred.

The essays thus draw out issues not visible in existing English-language translations of Rodríguez's work, which consist mostly of poetry (albeit poetry that slides into prose, destabilizing genre boundaries). *Other Letters to Milena* reveals her ongoing process of growth. Rodríguez, who first established her place in the Latin American literary scene as a poet, sought even in a moment of extreme social crisis to keep pushing her work in different directions in the new century. She moved through a variety of genres and interlocutors, deliberately, in order to revitalize her writing with greater depth and range. This artistic dynamism embodies an argument against assumptions that Cuban life has faltered or died amongst the post-Soviet ruins.

Other writers she cites in the essays provide her with alternative perspectives on the twentieth century, its arts, and its transitions from one state of existence to another. Nina Berberova's autobiography is a particularly good example. A document tracing her growing love and need for art, *The Italics Are Mine* opens with reflection after reflection on how Berberova's trajectory toward writing overlapped with vast historical

change. As an adolescent, Berberova remembers, she couldn't foresee the transformations to come: "I did not guess that I would belong to that generation for whom the old state of things would end" (49).

There Is Only Diaspora

In *Other Letters to Milena*, diaspora becomes capacious enough to describe artistic conditions of alienation: alienation from a self, from an imagined home for which one longs, from a community imagined in the process of tremendous change, from a projected home toward which one steps even while questioning that trajectory. All of these forms of distance produce the gap Rodríguez marks between poetic language and reality. While I was working on this translation, a series of events drove home the most literal, heart-wrenching elements of the book, illustrating how contemporary territorial Cuba intertwines with Cuban America and other diasporic Americas here in the United States.

After years of frustration Rodríguez finally received permits to travel to the United States in the spring of 2010 for a professional visit, presenting her work at the Instituto Cervantes and several campuses in the New York City area. We met in Brooklyn with Joel Kuszai, a professor at Queensborough Community College and our editor at Factory School, who brought several of his students to meet us. Rodríguez asked them questions about themselves, listened to their stories, and urged them to see themselves as writers. The next day we went to their campus to give a bilingual reading. After these events, instead of concentrating on translations in progress as previously planned, we talked about her strong reaction to the stories students had shared about their families and migrations. Rodríguez remarked on a young man from Africa, a young woman from Trinidad. She was especially overcome by speaking with two young women who were born in the Dominican Republic and had moved to the United States as children: neither one had seen her mother for seven years. One young woman seemed on the verge of tears when she spoke of her family. The other projected the stoic face of a survivor who must care for a younger sibling no matter what the circumstances may be.

Just before Rodríguez began this 2010 trip to the United States, she had attended a wedding in Havana. Her daughter, Elis Milena, then approximately the same age as the two Dominican students from Queensborough Community College, married a young man with whom she had grown up. It was only a matter of months before Elis would leave Havana for a new life in Miami, where her husband had already established a home.

In some ways Elis Milena has remained close to her mother since making her journey, settling within the orbit of the thriving south Florida community, which retains close ties to the island. Sporadic return visits to the island are likely for her, and Rodríguez has been able to visit her in Florida, hoping that more professional invitations will make additional visits possible in the future, always pending permission from governments. In the meantime they can communicate fairly regularly by email (though rationing has restricted access on the Cuban side). Still Elis is a world apart in the rhythms of everyday life, distanced from her family by the costs, restrictions, and pain of the long-term political opposition that widens the gap between the cities. She is making a new life for herself in a world with different challenges and prospects. This was one of the many possibilities foretold by the book Rodríguez named for her daughter.

Each time I've translated a book of poetry, some unexpected overlap has appeared. In this case, I had no idea when I started work on *Other Letters to Milena* that Elis Milena's journey to the United States would be happening, let alone coinciding so absolutely with the journey of her mother's writing into English. This coincidence not only created unexpected emotions around my work with the book and set up potential sensitivities as we spoke about its contents, but emphasized a whole layer of the book's subject matter: the profound impact of separation on family life. Rodríguez will surely have readers who relate to parts of this book work not because of their interest in Cuba's historical status or dialogues on post-Soviet life, but because of their own difficult experiences of transition.

In the end diaspora is what it is. In *Other Letters to Milena* it's also much more, and much less: diaspora flattens into a horizon between life and death. I am reminded of remarks by Anna Veltfort, after whom writer Lourdes Casal (also Cuban) named a famous 1976 poem about exile in New York. "Lourdes understood the universality of exile," Veltfort told interviewers, describing the meaning of that exile as "a universal sorrow" (Negrón-Muntaner 67).

Havana, Miami, Vienna, Niagara Falls, St. Petersburg, a concentration camp, women alive and dead, Beckett's ruins, entangled nations, some however many sheets of paper: there is no one Milena and no singular location where she resides: the message is messier, its lettering motion.

Kristin Dykstra

Works Cited

Beckett, Samuel. *The Complete Short Prose, 1929–1969*. Ed. and int. S. E. Gontarski. NY: Grove, 1995.

Behar, Ruth. "After the Bridges." In *The Portable Island: Cubans at Home in the World*. Ruth Behar and Lucía M. Suárez, eds. NY: Palgrave MacMillan, 2008. 3–8.

Berberova, Nina. *The Italics Are Mine*. Tr. Philippe Radley. NY: Harcourt, Brace, and World, 1969.

Birkenmaier, Anke, and Esther Whitfield, eds. *Havana beyond the Ruins: Cultural Mappings after 1989*. Durham, NC: Duke University Press, 2011.

Blanchot, Maurice. *The Writing of the Disaster*, 1980. Tr. Ann Smock. Lincoln: University of Nebraska Press, 1995.

Bobes, Velia Cecilia. "Visits to a Non-Place: Havana and Its Representation(s)." In Birkenmaier and Whitfield, 15–30.

Buckwalter-Arias, James. "Reinscribing the Aesthetic: Cuban Narrative and Post-Soviet Cultural Politics." *PMLA* 120:2 (Mar. 2005): 362–374. Web. JSTOR.

Cerna, Jana. *Kafka's Milena*, 1969. Tr. A. G. Brain. Evanston, IL: Northwestern UP, 1993.

Cortina, Rodolfo J. "History and Development of Cuban American Literature: A Survey." In *Handbook of Hispanic Cultures in the United States: Literature and Art*, vol. 3. Francisco Lomelí, ed.; Nicolás Kanellos and Claudio Estava-Fabregat, gen. eds. Houston: Arte Público Press, 1993. 40–61.

De los Angeles Torres, María. "Transnational Political and Cultural Identities: Crossing Theoretical Borders." In *Latino Thought: Culture, Politics, and Society*. Francisco H. Vázquez and Rodolfo D. Torres, eds. Lanham, MD: Rowman and Littlefield Publishers, 2003.

García, María Cristina. *Havana USA: Cuban Exiles and Cuban Americans in South Florida, 1959–1994*. Berkeley: University of California Press, 1996.

Gibian, George. "Who Was Milena?" In Cerna, 1–23.

Gruesz, Kirsten Silva. *Ambassadors of Culture: The Transamerican Origins of Latino Writing*. Princeton, NJ: Princeton University Press, 2002.

Gutiérrez, José Ismael. "Más allá de la homotextualidad: *Antes que anochezca*," de Reinaldo Arenas. *Revista de Estudios Hispánicos* 39.1 (Jan. 2005): 101–127. Web. Humanities International Complete.

Hernández Reguant, Ariana, ed. *Cuba in the Special Period: Culture and Ideology in the 1990s*. NY: Palgrave MacMillan, 2009.

Kafka, Franz. *Letters to Milena*. Tr. and int. Philip Boehm. NY: Schocken Books, 1990.

Lazo, Rodrigo. *Writing to Cuba: Filibustering and Cuban Exiles in the United States*. Chapel Hill: University of North Carolina Press, 2005.

Loss, Jacqueline. "Wandering in Russian." In Hernández Reguant, 105–122.

Negrón-Muntaner, Frances, and Yolanda Martínez-San Miguel. "In Search of Lourdes Casal's 'Ana Veldford.'" *Social Text* 92 (25.3, Fall 2007): 57–84.

O'Reilly Herrera, Andrea. *Cuban Artists Across the Diaspora: Setting the Tent against the House.* Austin: University of Texas Press, 2011.

Ortiz, Ricardo. "Revolution's Other Histories: The Sexual, Cultural, and Critical Legacies of Roberto Fernández Retamar's 'Caliban.'" *Social Text* 58 (Spring 1999): 33–58. Web. JSTOR.

Quiroga, José. "Bitter Daiquiris." In Birkenmaier and Whitfield, 270–285.

Padilla, Heberto. "In Hard Times." Tr. Jorge Guitart. In *The Cuba Reader: History, Culture, Politics.* Aviva Chomsky, Barry Carr, and Pamela Maria Smorkaloff, eds. Durham, NC: Duke University Press, 2004. 488–489.

Rodríguez, Reina María. "'Como de camino hacia un parque:' Conversando con Reina María Rodríguez" (interview with Julio Ramos, Francisco Morán, and Nestor Rodríguez). *La Habana Elegante, Segunda Época* Fall/Winter 2010. n.p. Web. http://www.habanaelegante.com/Fall_Winter_2010/Entrevista_Rodriguez.html

——————————. *La detención del tiempo / Time's Arrest*, Ed. and trans. Kristin Dykstra, 2nd ed. NY: Factory School, 2005.

——————————. *Otras cartas a Milena.* City of Havana, Cuba: Ediciones UNIÓN, 2003.

——————————. Personal conversations with the author. Havana, Cuba: June 3 and 8, 2010.

——————————. *Violet Island and Other Poems.* Trans. Kristin Dykstra and Nancy Gates Madsen. Los Angeles: Green Integer, 2004.

A Note on the Text

For this English-language edition of her book, Reina María Rodríguez and I opted to leave out some minor texts originally included in the Spanish-language edition from Cuba. This is because she didn't see the pieces as essential to that edition. Her publisher in Cuba thought the original manuscript for *Otras cartas a Milena* was too short, so she agreed to add some extra texts. Here we've dropped the extras in order to restore her initial, more streamlined vision for the book.

At her request I also replaced her original version of the essay, "Bishops," with the revised version published in her book *Variedades de Galiano*.

Other Letters to Milena / Otras cartas a Milena

Elis Milena. Family photograph provided by Reina María Rodríguez.
Rephotographed at the author's home in Havana by Kristin Dykstra, 2010.

Duda

Te rodearán las altas montañas
de ese antiguo país al que siempre has temido.
Te rodearán para salvarte
de perecer en la insensatez.

Viaje otra vez al mundo perdido
—con nostalgia doble
y la razón abolida.
Viaje sin destino (para quienes quitaron de antemano
los parámetros de sobrevivir).

Él no era más que un muchacho untado en brea
que chapoteaba y chapoteaba en el alquitrán.
Una comezón en la garganta.

Lo rodearán altos pinos de insatisfacción:
años caídos con pliegues ocultos, dobleces.
¿Habrá desperdiciado la ocasión
por la solidez de una resaca?

Doubt

They'll crowd around you: high mountains
from the ancient country you've always feared.
They'll crowd around to rescue you
from dying of senselessness.

Journey to the lost world one more time
—your nostalgia doubled
reason abolished.
Journey with no destination (for those who got rid of
survival parameters, in advance).

He was just a boy dipped in pitch
splashing around and around in tar.
An itch in a throat.

Tall pines will crowd around him in dissatisfaction:
years felled with hidden folds, deceitfulness.
Has he missed his chance
because the undertow was too strong?

Paso de nubes

Arca de Noé: embarcación grande en que se salvaron del diluvio Noé y su familia y cierto número de animales. Caja de madera; depósito para recibir el agua; depósito en que se guardaban las tablas de la ley; cajón o sitio donde se encierran varias cosas...

Aquí también se encierran varias cosas. Destinos. Posibilidades. Templos y palacios. Columnas y obeliscos; pirámides y zigurat movidos hacia el agua. Bautizos (iconografías) otra plástica de bulto—como en el antiguo arte—más allá de la isla de Argos. Los movimientos parecen torpes. Los relieves que cubrían la realidad, o las paredes (un hombre semiyaciente en medio de la arena). Es también la estatua yaciente de un hombre Meroe. La pirámide es una pirámide de balsas. Una balsa trae una muñeca recostada a los remos. También hay un caballo que acecha desde la orilla, si subirá o no esta vez la marea. Él los ve alejarse, aumentando el tamaño y la dimensión de sus figuras, alejarse y perderse en el confín del horizonte. Los niños siempre han jugado a las balsas, que zozobran y vuelven a flotar cuando el peso de las manos desaparece. Pero esta vez, las balsas suben y se ocultan del brazo que pretende sujetarlas—y una nube, como si fuera a saltar toda el agua blanca de la espuma derramada—se une al brazo del muchacho, despidiéndolas. Algunas se hundirán para siempre entre la arena y la resaca; otras tocarán el límite. Siempre sospecharemos cuál encalló, cuál regresó, la que habrá llegado. Es una Isla, con sus niños que han jugado, al crecer, con sus balsas. Mucha gente mojada con el agua hasta el pecho está rezando adentro. Veo los ojos de la niña, el tiovivo flotante donde van sus hermanos, la desolación. Se ha ido mi muñeca más querida también. Y aquella balsa—ataúd del centro, con un viejo siempre de espaldas a mi cámara, no quiere volver los pies y despedirse—es el abuelo. Balsas de madera, asfalto y poliespuma. Cristo delante de la caravana—un cuadro realista del Sagrado Corazón de Jesús—como proa. O esta otra, con una cruz de palo como mástil, que pasa enfrentándose al vaivén del vacío del viento. Laterales de zinc y goma, caucho recalentado. Un niño y una nube—un caballo también que se aproxima y bebe un sol salobre—han visto, cómo todos los otros se van y se pierden detrás de un límite impreciso.

Passage of Clouds

Noon (18 September 1994)

Noah's Ark: great embarkation in which Noah and his family, and a certain number of animals, were saved from the deluge. Wooden box; receptacle for collecting water; receptacle for safeguarding tablets of the law; crate or space in which various things are enclosed...

Here too various things are enclosed. Destinies. Possibilities. Temples and palaces. Columns and obelisks; pyramids and ziggurat blurring toward choppy water. Baptisms (iconographies), another art of a form—as in ancient sculpture—from beyond the island city of Argos. Their motion appears ungainly. Reliefs that filled reality, or the walls (a man semi-reclining in the sand); the reclining statue of a Meroitic man. The pyramid is a pyramid of boats. One raft carries a doll leaning on the oars. And at the coastline a horse waits to see whether the tide will rise or not this time. He sees them moving away into the distance, the size and dimension of their figures expanding as they get farther away, disappearing into the horizon's confine. The children have always played by rafts, which capsize and re-surface as the weight of their hands pulls away. But this time, the rafts rise and evade the arm that attempts to restrain them—and as if all the white water were about to fly out in spilling foam, a cloud adheres to the arm of the boy seeing them off. Some boats will sink for good between the sand and the undertow; others will touch up against the line of limitation. We'll always have our suspicions about the one that ran aground, the one that came back, the one that made land. This is an Island; the children grew up playing with its rafts. Many people soaked up to the chest with water are praying on the island. I see the girl's eyes, the floating carousel where her brothers have gone, the desolation. My favorite doll is gone too. And that raft—shroud at the center, with an old man whose back is always to my camera, who doesn't want to turn his feet to leave—it's the grandfather. Boats of wood, asphalt and Styrofoam. Christ at the front of the caravan—a realist painting of the Sacred Heart of Jesus—at the bow. Or this other one, a cross made of sticks for a mast, passes by, off to confront the rolling of the void in the wind. Sides of zinc and rubber, melted tire. A boy and a cloud—and a horse, who approaches to drink from a brackish sun— have seen how all the others go off, lost behind some vague boundary.

El pulpo

En el principio, la Diosa de todas las Cosas, surgió desnuda del Caos, pero no encontró nada sólido en qué apoyar los pies, y en consecuencia separó el mar del firmamento y danzó solitaria sobre las olas. Se dio la vuelta y se apoderó de ese viento norte, lo frotó entre sus manos…

De allí partió el "Galeón de Fernanda" que fue remolcado por un Chevrolet hasta la playa, hacia el atardecer. Fragmentos de una luz violeta y roja entre los matorrales. Las pisadas se han borrado por el viento norte que la Diosa de todas las Cosas trajo y después se perdieron (las cosas, las pisadas). Pero el pulpo es capaz de recordar y capitalizar sus recuerdos. El caballo se estremece con el olor a pulpo en la noche —una peregrinación hacia la nada; una peregrinación hacia el fondo del mar: esquizofrenia de la necesidad—bultos y formas inhumanas que el pulpo desde su horrible corola succiona. Se mantiene de pie como un hombre, su cabeza encapuchada, sus ojos enormes, su voluptuosidad de verdugo. Toda esta noche ha quedado grabada, succionada, por la cabeza del pulpo en la costa. Se esconde y espía. El arácnido marino ha sentido el golpe de la peregrinación hacia la nada, hacia la profunda soledad. Él también teme y recuerda "La cruzada de los niños". (El caballo no quiere volver a mirar lo que acontece, evita la total oscuridad que se aproxima, y huye.) Las voces, los gritos, los quejidos, las risas, los rezos, los ladridos van hacia la ruta del Tao.

Al amanecer, algunos fragmentos que el pulpo rechazó desde sus ojos enormes han regresado a la playa. El mal y el mar son inocentes (otra vez recuerdo a Baudelaire "con la verdad enfática del gesto" en las grandes circunstancias de la vida).

The Octopus

In the beginning the Goddess of all Things sprang naked from Chaos,
but she found nothing solid on which to place her feet. Consequently she
divided ocean from firmament and danced off alone across the waves.
Turning again she seized the north wind, kneaded it between her hands...

From there, "Fernanda's Galleon" departed, towed by a Chev-
rolet toward the beach, toward sunset. Shards of violet and red light
through thickets. The footsteps have been erased by the north wind,
which the Goddess of all Things brought, and then they were lost (they:
the things, the steps). But the octopus is capable of remembering, and
capable of compounding its memories. The horse shudders at the smell
of octopus in the night—a pilgrimage toward the void; a pilgrimage to-
ward the bottom of the sea; schizophrenia born of necessity—inhuman
shapes and forms that the octopus sucks in. It holds itself like a man,
standing, its head hooded, eyes giant, an executioner's voluptuousness.
This entire night has been recorded, sucked in, by the head of the
octopus at the coastline. It hides, it spies. The marine arachnid has felt
the blow of the pilgrimage toward nothingness, toward deep solitude. It
too fears and remembers "the children's crusade." (The horse does not
want to look back at what takes place, avoids the encroachment of total
darkness, flees.) The voices, shouts, moans, laughter, prayers, barking,
all go the way of the Tao.

At daybreak some fragments that the octopus had repelled from
its gigantic eyes return to the beach. Evil and the ocean are innocent
(again I remember Baudelaire's "emphatic truth of gesture" in the great
circumstances of life).

El mascarón

El mascarón de proa es un indio. El hombre que mira hacia atrás—hacia el amanecer—está todavía entre la ilusión y la playa; entre el deseo y la realidad; en un punto intermedio entre la razón y la sinrazón… "un sujeto que se bambolea entre dos lenguajes, expresivo el uno, crítico el otro …" Pero no voy a juzgarlo. La pirámide de verde lona y el indio, van de nuevo a conquistar otras tierras. Es la balsa de los locos, de los desesperados que intentan desafiar al pez con una cabeza de tiburón dibujada en la proa, "perro no come perro"—me señala. Parten de Cojímar, de Guanabo, de Santa Fe, de la mismísima bahía de La Habana. La escenografía de fondo es un faro, el Morro, la Cabaña. Desde las azoteas gritan a coro otras voces y bailan una danza macabra, se agitan pedazos de camisas, trapos… Ta ba sa (frente a frente) grita otra vez aquel niño en sánscrito. Entre la multitud encuentro el día, y los hombros de estos hombres que antes no existían para mí. Al amanecer, el indio que se aleja de su playa ve la fila de brazos que caen al agua; de rodillas que se inclinan para hacer su ofrenda a Yemayá pidiéndole permiso para cruzar el mar. (La diosa de todas las Cosas se los ha concedido.) Velas con sacos y rituales de iniciación al amanecer: triunfo del mito. La extrañeza como punto de partida; la vuelta a un tipo de mentalidad donde no existe entre la acción y el objetivo que se le señala, conexión de ninguna clase. Extrañeza de los fenómenos primitivos con los que acechamos también el azar. Sabemos que tienen estratos muy antiguos (Taylor ha introducido para tales manifestaciones el término de *supervivance*). *Supervivencias.* ¿Qué es, en general, lo que hace que una manifestación cultural adquiera el carácter de razonable? Interpretación prelógica de la bendición y la maldición (siempre que han sido bendecidos, a la vez son malditos). La verdadera causa alude al mundo de los poderes siempre ocultos y para esto, el conocimiento de la ley natural es un sentido. ¿Por qué no? La supervivencia es el único estímulo real de la forma en la especie.

The Figurehead

The boat's figurehead is an Indian. The man who looks back—toward sunrise—is poised still between illusion and beach; between desire and reality; at an intermediary point between reason and injustice... "a subject wobbling between two languages, the one expressive, the other critical..." But I will not judge him. The pyramid of green canvas and the Indian: they'll conquer new lands all over again. It's the ship of fools, the desperate, who try to scare off fish by drawing a shark's head on the prow—"dog doesn't eat dog," he tells me. They put in at Cojímar, at Guanabo, Santa Fe, at the bay of Havana itself. The background scenery consists of a lighthouse, the Morro castle, the fortress of San Carlos de La Cabaña. From the rooftops other voices shout, a chorus, and perform a macabre dance, they wave shreds of clothing, cloths... Ta ba sa (face to face), the boy cries again, in Sanskrit. Within the multitude I find the day, and the shoulders of these men who didn't exist for me before. At dawn, the Indian moving away from his beach sees the row of arms falling to the water; the row of knees bending to make their offerings to Yemayá, asking her permission to cross the sea. (The Goddess of all Things granted hers.) Sails from sacks, rituals of initiation at sunrise: the triumph of myth. Surprise as a point of departure; the return to a kind of mentality in which there is no connection of any kind between an action and the objective it indicates. The wonder of primitive phenomena, phenomena on which we too rely, waiting to learn our fate. We know they rest on ancient strata (for expressions like these, Taylor introduced the term *supervivance*). *Survivorships*. In general, what causes a form of cultural expression to acquire the status of a reasonable act? Pre-logical interpretation of blessing and curse (those who have been blessed have always been cursed at the same time). The true cause refers back to the world of perpetually occult powers and for this, knowledge of natural law is a form of attentiveness. Why not? Survivorshop is the only real stimulus shaping the species.

El fotógrafo

El fotógrafo nos enseña cómo se corre detrás del peligro. Se monta en el invento de embarcación y coloca su cámara que vuelve a ser anzuelo y sal. Llega con los náufragos hasta el horizonte. Yo lo persigo. ¿Quién podría guiarme? "Lo que la fotografía reproduce al infinito únicamente ha tenido lugar una sola vez." Esa sola vez suficiente para germinar. El fotógrafo es actor y espectador en el espacio de su foto. No puede juzgar. Participa. El fotógrafo no tiene ideología preexistente, es acto, y su acción se antepone a cualquier verbalización, o discurso. El fotógrafo es un espectro, un fantasma que se corporiza en la mirada del ojo. Es el ojo el que ve, y ya no hay habla. Yo lo persigo. Mientras se monta en su cámara común y goza con el desenfreno del horror. Su vigilia es constante. Ha restaurado con esa foto, el cuadro que dejó en la exposición inconcluso: ha rematado el toque final de su pincel contra el tiempo—esta es su heroicidad—, consumir a cada instante, en cada clic, un rostro, un cuerpo, un naufragio. También él es el pulpo, el otro pulpo. Pasa de una tonalidad a otra, según la emotividad. Dos ojos anchos y oscuros con las pupilas dilatadas de los ojos verdaderos, recreándose. Entre la noche y el día, un pulpo que espía desde el mar y un pulpo diurno (el pulpo diurno es el pulpo de esta partida). Los dos han tragado las imágenes con sal (antropofagia de la imagen). Son dos cazadores por oposición que regresan a contarnos la historia de un hombre que se perdió en el mar… De un tumulto que se perdió en el mar.

The Photographer

The photographer shows us how to pursue danger. Spurring the craft
of fabrication he situates his camera, which turns to bait and salt, as it
has before. Among shipwrecked people, the photographer arrives at the
horizon. I chase after him. Who could guide me? "The thing that photog-
raphy infinitely reproduces has taken place on one single occasion." That
single occasion sufficient for germination. The photographer is an actor
and a spectator inside the space of his photograph. He can't judge. He
participates. The photographer has no pre-existing ideology; he is an act,
and his action precedes verbalization or speech. The photographer is a
specter, a ghost who materializes in the eye through its gaze. It's the eye
that sees, and there is no more speech. I chase after him. While he sets
up his camera and revels in abandonments of horror. His vigil is con-
stant. With that photograph, he restored a painting he had left unfinished
in the exhibition: he gave his final touch to time—this is his form of
heroism—consuming in every instant, with every click, a face, a body, a
shipwreck. He too is the octopus, the other octopus. He transitions from
one tonality to another, according to the emotion of the scene. Two wide,
dark eyes and the pupils of the truest eyes, dilated with the pleasures of
recreating. Between the night and the day, one octopus spying from the
sea and another octopus, diurnal (the diurnal one is here in this entry).
The two have swallowed their images with salt (cannibalism of the im-
age). They're two opposed hunters, returning to tell us the story about a
man who was lost at sea ... about a commotion that was lost at sea.

El cuento de la niña

Teníamos una casa alquilada para pasar unos días en la playa (era la primera vez que pasaríamos unos días en la playa, juntos). Pero la niña—de cinco años entonces—me dijo que no quería ir al mar porque tenía miedo de encontrar alguna cosa: una pierna, un brazo, un corazón, algo desgarrado o mutilado entre las algas. Pensé mucho en esa "marca de agua" en el mar. También en los bañistas y en el frágil muro donde nos sentábamos de espaldas al olor de la resaca. La ciudad es lo que vemos y lo que está sumergido es doble como su transparencia. El agua que delimita la otra orilla siempre está por detrás y por debajo, adentrándose. Es un mar que no miramos, pero que reaparece en cada bocacalle. Reaparece y se esconde, para exigirnos su visión. Pensé en las algas enredadas a restos humos de un paisaje, y sentí las exigencias de ese mar, su maremoto. Desde entonces, no he vuelto a mirarlo.

I

Querida hija, estoy de regreso. No me fui, tal vez, no me voy. Me esperaban en Viena alguna fama, algún dinero, algunas personas que quiero. ¿Así que realmente no fuiste a Viena? ¿No fuiste a Viena?, ¿no fuiste a Viena? —le pregunta Kafka a Milena. Pero esos aeropuertos con personas a las que nada puedes preguntar. Si preguntas, ¿vas para Viena? Te responden Oslo, o cualquier otro lugar. Todos se sienten perseguidos y te despistan (yo también). Estoy escapándome frente al antiguo Rivoli, ahora sólo fachada. Lo peor es que aquí también soy una extraña. Ver esta destrucción y pensar que se puede escapar fácilmente es una falacia. Mi avión andará surcando el cielo (eso me parece una malísima metáfora). Yo aquí, detenida entre el perderlo todo y regresar. Este horror constante entre el sangrar y el vacío. ¿Qué palabra puede reemplazar esta angustia, mi pobre imaginario perseguido por algunas constantes de mí? No soy Simonne Well, la mística judía, que comía la misma ración de pan de los concentrados para mantener su fe. Cuando estoy, Milena, en este tránsito, siento el peor de los abismos: no estoy allá, pero tampoco estoy aquí. (Porque, yo huí del consciente de mí hace mucho tiempo y, ahora, sólo me queda estar partida entre dos túneles.) Esa esquizofrenia galopante; esa dualidad de ser algo parecido a ti y, su representación; esa fuerza que me empuja a ser... "un demás" y, esa otra que me permite creerme un "yo". Hija mía, lo que está destruido no está afuera, sino dentro del cerebro del hombre,

The Girl's Story

We had rented a house to spend a few days at the beach (it was the first time we'd spend a few days at the beach together). But my daughter— then five years old—told me she didn't want to go to the ocean because she was afraid of finding something in the seaweed: a leg, an arm, a heart, something torn off or mutilated. I thought a lot about this "watermark" on the ocean. And about swimmers, and the fragile wall where we sat with our backs to the smell of undertow. The city is what we see, and that which is submerged is double-sided, like the reflection's transparency. Water that defines the other shore is always moving, deep inside, behind and below. We don't look at this ocean, but it reappears at the end of every street. It reappears and conceals itself to demand that we see it. I thought about seaweed twining through the smoky remains of a land- scape, and I felt the demands from that ocean, its oceanquake. Since then, I haven't gone back to look any more.

I

My dear daughter, I came back. I didn't go, maybe, I'm not going. Some fame, some money, some people I love were waiting for me in Vienna. So you really didn't go to Vienna? You didn't go to Vienna? you didn't go to Vienna?—Kafka asks Milena. But those airports, with people you can't ask about anything. If you ask, are you going to Vienna?, they reply Oslo, or whatever other place. Everyone feels persecuted and shakes you off (including me). I'm fleeing past the old Rivoli, now only a façade. The worst part is that here I'm a stranger too. To see this destruction and think you can easily escape is a fallacy. My airplane will plow through the sky (that looks like a terrible metaphor to me). Me here, suspended be- tween losing it all and going back. This constant horror between bleeding out and the void. What word can replace this anguish, my poor imaginary persecuted by my routines for myself? I'm not Simone Weil, the Jewish mystic who ate the same ration of bread as the people in concentration camps in order to maintain her faith. Milena, when I'm in this transit, I know the worst of the abysses: I'm not there, but I'm not here either. (Because I fled self-awareness long ago and now, I'm left divided between two tunnels.) That galloping schizophrenia; that duality, to be some- thing resembling you, and its representation; the force that pushes me to be… "a remainder" and another woman, who permits me to believe myself a "self." Daughter, the thing destroyed is not outside, but inside the human brain; the more effort it makes, the more the brain can live

13

que por más esfuerzos que haga vive su mito como si fuera la verdad, y no puede comprender. Sólo hay diáspora... Oigo tu voz en mi oído, tu mano pequeña y caliente entre mis dedos —"no te vayas", me dices. ¿Qué puedo hacer por ti? Recuerdo esa película de Fellini, donde el intelectual asesina a sus dos hijos por miedo a dejarlos aquí; el miedo al escándalo de vivir esta representación sin respuesta...

No llego a Viena —no llego a ninguna parte. Soy un ser del tránsito, de los trayectos, de los procesos, no de la finalidad. Me monto en un carro donde, de tantas personas, me falta el aire... Hablo dos horas con un desconocido, en un parque cerca del Capitolio... La noche va cayendo sobre mí, y entre sus sombras, la luna —como una fiera de regreso— sale por detrás del miedo, y me alumbra: alumbra mi ilusión de ser perdida entre esta nada de mi pobre imaginario que ni siquiera puede cambiar, ni puede concebir, una visión más moderna del dolor...

La Habana, febrero de 1994

II

"Quiero amarte, quiero amar a alguien que pueda fundir esta dispersión en un haz, pero ya no es posible." Llego a este otro lado —de mi recuerdo, de mi pasado— un pueblito en cuaresma, con calor y polvo de domingo de ramos (ya sé que no habrá resurrección). Dejo una pucha de flores moradas entre las rejas del patio —se van a caer—, sé que este viento se las va a llevar. La iglesia está cerrada y tocan las campanas para un pueblo sordo. Las casas de madera, también a punto de caer sobre pilotes de yeso. Parece una tierra de nadie. Tú estás allí, y él también. Pero aquella quietud y austeridad de la miseria que lo hace a todo carente de metafísica, ¿las podré soportar? Quiero huir de mi recuerdo y saltar mi propia imposibilidad humana hasta cansarme de que todo ocurra sin trascendencia (porque a esta cacharrería de palabras que se llamó "literatura", yo quise darle objeto de existencia y, ella también me engaña). Y entre los túneles me travestizo. Huyo por el hueco negro del simulacro, edulcoro la letra, el discurso y la pasión. Me "engolo" para no aceptar —y, esa mediocridad con la que escondo mi cuerpo que empieza a envejecer debajo de las sábanas; esa mediocridad con la que cierro los ojos para no ver tu otro ojo azul (su aro amarillo) al regresar, en la noche, a otra cama, a otro tiempo, a otros brazos, que son tal vez más rígidos, pero también más constantes...

Pueblito de postal. Y, en ella —no inmersa, sólo detenida, paralizada por el terror— yo, que no vivo, que añoro y detesto vivir de

out its myth as if that were truth, and it cannot understand. There is only diaspora... I hear your voice in my ear, your small warm hand between my fingers—"don't go," you tell me. What can I do for you? I remember that Fellini film where the intellectual murders his two children for fear of leaving them here; the fear of scandal, of living out this representation with no reply...

I don't get to Vienna—I don't get anywhere. I'm a being of transit, of trajectories, processes, not finality. I get into a car with so many other people that I have no air to breathe... I spend two hours talking to a stranger in a park near the Capitol... Night goes on falling over me, and between its shadows, the moon—like a wild animal making its way home—moves out from behind fear and illuminates me: illuminates my illusion of being lost in the nothingness of my impoverished imaginary; it can't change, can't conceive of a more modern angle on the pain...

Havana, February 1994

II

"I want to love you, want to love someone who could meld this diffusion into a beam." I arrive at this other side—of my memory, of my past—a little town during Lent, with the heat and dust of Palm Sunday (I already know there won't be a resurrection). I leave a bouquet of purple flowers between bars of the window on the patio—they're going to fall—I know this wind will take them. The church is closed and bells ring for a deaf *pueblo*. Wooden homes, also about to fall down, on piles of plaster. It looks like an empty land. You're there, and so is he. But that stillness, and the austerity of misery which cuts metaphysics out of everything: will I be able to bear them? I want to flee my memory and leap out of my human impossibility, until I'm worn down by this fact that everything can happen without transcendence (because I wanted to give this hardware store of words called "literature" a purpose for existing, and it deceived me too). And among tunnels I put on other identities. I flee through the black hole of simulacrum, sweeten the word, the discourse, passion. I "enlist" so as not to accept—and that mediocrity under which I hide my body, which begins to age under the bedsheets; that mediocrity with which I cover my eyes, so as not to see your other blue eye (its yellow ring) when I return at night to a different bed, another time, other arms that may be more rigid but also more constant...

Little postcard town. And in her, not immersed, just detained, paralyzed by terror—I, who am not living, who yearns to live and hates it from wanting it so much; I write my first letter to you, the possibility

tanto quererlo, escribo una primera carta para ti, que eres una posible mujer (otra Milena) que tampoco huirá de su campo de concentración, su útero, del que no hay puerta oblicua para escapar. Dos bordes estrechos y en el centro, tú (aquella, la otra). Ese instante de saber que somos obra, prefabricación constante, y que esa obra mustia, o salpicada de sombras de yeso, también tiene que morir por su precio, su bajo precio de acontecer. "Vivir es imposible"—dice ella, S.W.—frente a la fachada del Rivoli, donde alguien cantó, alguna vez. Ahora escombros y piedras que lo arrastran todo. Pobre pájaro, ese gorrión que sobrevive al incendio, aún quemado; pájaro de alas bajitas para resistir una existencia inicua, indiferente. Estoy loca por romper esta dualidad que nos abisma (tú, la llamas cobardía) cada vez más, dentro de un silencio de cuaresma, de un silencio que viene del sur y arrastra un polvo que también te lleva a ti…

"Leo un libro sobre el Tibet; al llegar a la descripción de un pueblo en las montañas de la frontera se me oprime de pronto el corazón, tan desolada y abandonada me parece la aldea, tan alejada de Viena. Pero lo que me parece estúpido es la idea de que el Tibet queda lejos de Viena. ¿Quedaría realmente lejos?…" (Kafka).

Aeropuerto
Santiago de las Vegas, 27 de marzo de 1994

III

El cielo que prende con su amarillo al atardecer, las casas; la bola encendida del sol contra el mar y esas palomas que se desplazan y quejan en círculos contra mi cuerpo. Llegan y se van. Me siento a mirar cómo has crecido—ya el muro te da bajo el vientre—y pareces sacada de un cuento, de una pradera tan verde y árida, como su desolación. Tu pelo que se dora en la tarde sobre la espalda (¡buena mezcla eres tú!). Saya de mezclilla azul y ojos asiáticos. Te quiero en la belleza que imaginé y no fui. Saber que no estaré luego, pasar la mano donde ha crecido otro detalle del cuadro. Ahora jugamos al teatro (si otra vez fuera pequeña como tú, correríamos paralelas al tren, sobre algo que corre, y que se escapa). Cruzas las piernas, te echas el pelo hacia atrás y, observas, que el cielo todavía está, tan azul y paralizado allí, que no se puede tocar ni comprender. Entonces, abro el libro de Silvia P. y busco "Picaduras"— ese poema que me enerva y me atiza la sangre.

He vuelto a descubrir, que no tengo lenguaje para pronunciar el círculo que la realidad ha hecho a mi alrededor. Pujo y vuelvo a estrechar el círculo. Abro la estructura entre un sustantivo y su fábula (me aprieto más). Nos dormimos cuando las sombras caen…

of woman (another Milena) who won't run away from her concentration camp either, her uterus, where there's no oblique exit for escape. Two thin edges and between them, you (that woman over there, the other one). The moment of knowing that we are the work, a continual prefabrication, and that the work, melancholic or spattered with shadows from plaster, also has to die to earn its price, the low price for its occurrence. "Life is impossible"—she says, S.W.—facing the Rivoli's façade, where somebody once sang. Now rubble and stones, they drag it all away. Poor bird, swallow that survives the fire, somewhat burnt; bird with short wings for beating off an unjust, indifferent existence. I'm desperate to crack this duality that plunges us (you, you call it cowardliness) ever deeper into a prescribed silence, into a silence that comes from the south carrying dust, carrying you along too...

"I'm reading a book about Tibet; when I get to the description of a border town in the mountains my heart suddenly grows heavy, so desolate and abandoned the village seems to me, so far from Vienna. But what I consider stupid is the idea that Tibet is far away from Vienna. Could it really be far?..." (Kafka).

Airport
Santiago de las Vegas, 27 March 1994

III

Sky bathing houses in yellow at sunset; flaming ball of sun against the sea and those doves, who complain as they circle back against my body. They come and go. I sit down to see how you've grown—the wall already hits below your belly button—and you look as though you were taken from a story, from a grassland green and arid as its desolation. Your hair that turns golden in the evening, over your back (a lovely blend you are!). Blue denim skirt and Asiatic eyes. I love you in beauty I imagined and was not. Knowing that I won't be here later, passing my hand over the place where another detail of the painting has grown. Now we're playing theater (if I were little again like you, we'd run together, parallel to the train, over something else that runs along and gets away). You cross your legs, throw your hair back, and observe: the sky is still so blue and paralyzed, there, that it can't be touched or understood. Then I open Sylvia Plath's book and look for "Stings"—a poem that irritates me and stirs my blood.

I've come to discover again that I have no language for delivering the circle, the one reality drew around me. I struggle and make the circle tighter. I open the structure between a noun and its fabula (squeezing myself more tightly). We drop off to sleep when shadows fall...

"Por la ventana abierta sobre el paisaje, los pinos, el sol que ha caído, las montañas, la aldea y por sobre todo una visión de Viena …" (Kafka). Tu vida devora a la mía. El sol ha bajado aún más y, yo me entrego reducida otra vez a la especie que no me provoca otra forma de fin, o de resurrección. Echamos bolitas de nuestro único pan a Diotima, a Dédalus, al pequeño Elias Canetti—ellos viven como humanos, en un mundo donde los humanos semejan su animal a la perfección, ¡sólo les falta sonreír! ¿Cómo trascender ese infinito azul sobre nuestras cabezas? Quisiera lanzarme contigo, antes de que toquen a la puerta, y el planeta que creé pueda volverse otra ilusión…

Regreso del sueño con el equipaje que viajó solo a Viena, tiene otro olor. La tembladera bajo mi saya, de un uniforme de soñar polvoriento (ya no hay leche, no hay nada). Trato de crear un performance triste de mi reencuentro con el equipaje, con la fe—¿qué se vuelve el objeto sin su lugar, sin mi posesión? Siento horror de estar tan sola entre los objetos. (Mi ropa de invierno está en el interior de ese maletín Prusia, tal vez, no volverá a ver la nieve.) Me hundo de nuevo en la tembladera y tomo un caldo de cabezas de pescado hirviendo. ¡Explotar todo este horror no puede ser la vida! El paisaje de afuera, caliente y árido, también me carcome por dentro, y monto un discurso (otra justificación) que no vale nada tampoco. Un cura pasa con su sotana negra, me hace levantar la mirada. Él, tan obsoleto como yo, y vuelvo a pensar en ti. ¡Ah, hija mía, qué débil y miserable es esto! No estoy en Livry, ni me paseo por la corte a través de dulces jardines, pero somos—como ellas—dos princesas escapadas de un cuento, a las que una hada mala castigó en el árido jardín.

Azotea, 5 de abril de 1994

IV

Anoche, podía soportar el ruido de mi soledad. Tocaba los objetos con los ojos húmedos y me alegraba de tenerlos, rodeándome. Pero nadie comprende, ni permite tu libertad. La falta de flexibilidad que proporciona el ego venció, y luego, poco a poco, la indiferencia.

Anoche, yo quería estar en la casita de brujas con sus jarros de cerámica, conversando como dos antiguas amigas (puede ser que agazape el resto de mis miedos en ti, el de ser la otra mujer). Pero hay días en los que sólo con despertar y salir contigo a caminar, al mismo lugar—como si fuera único—, bajo mis pies el aceite recalentado, el olor a petróleo que se pudre sin llegar al mar, me hacen caer contra la gravedad y ser verdaderamente humana y feliz. Ya no puedo—aunque me sobra morbo—mirar

"Through the window open to the landscape, the pines, the sun that has set, the mountains, the village and above all a vision of Vienna…" (Kafka). Your life devours mine. The sun sinks even further and I surrender, reduced again to the species that provokes no other form of ending, or resurrection. We toss tiny balls from our only loaf of bread to Diotima, Daedalus, little Elias Canetti—they live like humans, in a world where humans emulate their animal perfectly. Cats lack only a smile! How can we transcend this infinite blue above our heads? I'd like to leap off with you before they knock on the door and the planet I created collapses back into another illusion…

I return from dream with luggage that traveled to Vienna by itself; it has a different smell. Quivering under my skirt from the dusty dreaming uniform (now there's no milk, there's nothing). I try to create a sad performance of my re-encounter with the luggage, with faith—what does the object become without its place, without my possession of it? I feel horror at being so alone among objects. (My winter clothes are inside that Prussian-blue suitcase; maybe they'll never see that snow again.) I submerge into my trembling again and sip at a scalding broth of fish heads. Exploitation of all this horror—it can't be a life! The landscape outside, hot and arid, eats away at me on the inside too, and I assemble a discourse (another justification), worth nothing either. A priest passes by in his black cassock, causing me to lift my gaze. There he is, just as obsolete as I am, and I go back to thinking about you. Oh, my daughter, how weak and miserable this is! I'm not in Livry, not at the queen's court strolling through sweet gardens; instead we're two princesses—like them—escaped from a story, the ones punished by a bad fairy, in a garden that all dried up.

Rooftop, 5 April 1994

IV

Last night I was able to bear the noise of my solitude. I touched objects with moist eyes and felt happy to have them surrounding me. But no one understands or permits your freedom. The lack of flexibility that supplies the ego won out, and then, little by little, came indifference.

Last night I wanted to be inside the witches' cottage with their ceramic jars, chatting like two old friends (it might be that I'm lowering the rest of my fears into you, the fear about being the other woman). But there are days when it's only by waking up and going out to walk with you, to the same old place—as if it were special—under my feet: reheated cooking oil, smell of petroleum that rots before arriving at the sea, these induce me to contradict gravity with my fall, to be truly human and happy.

las caras, los hombros, las pieles que se cuartean y se caen. Te he traído a un campo minado, donde dentro de la propia conciencia está el peligro. (Nos caemos contra el cielo otra vez.) Tú me aprietas la mano, quieres un helado de fresa que no te puedo pagar. No hay guerra para justificar este desgaste. Buscamos la sombra azul. (Aún así, ¡soy feliz de la mano contigo!) Cuando te escondes entre las campanas, si tienes miedo te pegas a mí, que tengo más miedo que tú. Es como si el mal, la representación misma del mal, se hubiera encarnado en el paisaje y en la gente (como la víctima que encarna al diablo sin saberlo, y por eso es condenada).

Todas las brujas danzan alrededor de ti, de mí, de esta casa, de aquellas campanas, y nosotras en el centro—tan inocentes—, olvidamos que detrás de esas puertas hay orine de ratas que pueden contaminarnos ("los pies se contraen convulsivamente, uno está aterrado y no tiene nada que hacer, salvo contemplar las grandes ratas oscuras, su mirada deslumbrante en medio de la noche…"). Te hago vivir en el horror—ya que no hay tampoco alternativa sin él—y nadie puede huir de su cerebración ni se huye hacia ningún lugar.

Plaza de la Catedral, Habana Vieja, en la noche…

V

Mientras corres alrededor de la estatua y la tocas, preguntándome si hay alguien adentro—con tus tenis cuadriculados y la mochila prusia a la espalda—tratando de alcanzar algún pájaro de la rama de un árbol con una sola flor azul, te he visto años atrás, y años después, con la conciencia de no estar ya en ninguna parte—para recoger ese fruto que caerá, de la única flor sobre el pico del pájaro. Entonces, para cuando ya no esté y, hayas cazado tu pájaro inconcluso, leas esta carta como si estuviera contigo, en la dulce mañana de abril que será siempre nuestra. No sé cómo se llama esta parque, "tampoco habría podido perderte en aquel parque… " (Kafka), en las noches cuando se borra la silueta de una mujer que fui, mientras él me acariciaba. (Hoy vi que la estatua de la fuente blanca es la forma de una mujer que es sacada del agua por dos hombres, uno por el frente, el otro por la espalda, una alegoría.) Tracé una línea sobre lo real en diferentes bancos y, ahora, con la brisa que viene de Cojímar y resucita, más que mis recuerdos, el después, comprendo que la frontera me la creó cierta mediocridad para resistir tanta humedad en los labios. Hay también—como en el pomo de madera que he colocado en el centro de la mesa—sal, pan, y agua. Y, te bautizo en esta mañana de abril con flores azules (Novalis) que han caído de otro pequeño árbol, para cuando vuelvas a correr alrededor cazando

Now—despite being excessively morbid—I can't look at faces, shoulders, skins that crack and fall off. I've brought you into a minefield, where danger lies inside one's own consciousness. (We fall back into the sky again.) You squeeze my hand, you want strawberry ice cream I can't afford to buy. There's no war to justify this debilitation. We search for the blue shadow. (Even like this, I'm happy holding your hand!) When you hide between bells, if you're scared, you press up against me, when I'm more scared than you. It's as though evil, the very representation of evil, had become incarnate in landscape and people (like the victim who is the devil incarnate but doesn't know it, and is condemned).

All the witches are dancing around you, me, this house, those bells, and at the center—so innocent—we forget that behind those doors is urine from rats who could contaminate us ("feet contract convulsively, you panic and there's nothing you can do but contemplate the great dark rats, their gaze blinding in the middle of the night…"). I cause you to live in horror—now there's no alternative without it—and no one can flee their own cerebration, or fly toward any place.

Cathedral Plaza, Old Havana, nighttime…

V

As you run around the statue, touching it, asking me if there's anyone inside—with your square-toe sneakers and dark blue pack on your back—trying to reach some bird on the branch of a tree with a single blue flower, I've seen you years earlier, and years later, with the sensation of being nowhere at all—trying to pick up the fruit, which will fall from the singular flower onto the bird's beak. So when I might no longer be here, and maybe you'll have captured your inconclusive bird, you may read this letter as if I were there with you, on the sweet April morning that will always belong to us. I don't know what this park is called, "nor could I lose you in that distant park" (Kafka), in the night when the silhouette blurs, the woman I was, while he caressed me. (Today I saw that the statue in the white fountain has the shape of a woman pulled from water by two men, one in front, one in back, an allegory.) On different benches I traced a line over the real and now, with the breeze that blows in from Cojímar and resuscitates more than my memories, something that came afterwards, I understand that the border created for me a certain mediocrity, to withstand so much moisture on my lips. There are also—in the wooden jar I set down on the center of the table—salt, bread, and water. And I baptize you on this April morning with blue flowers (Novalis) fallen from another small tree, for when you start running around again,

pájaros. Sé que al irme, me quedaré otra vez dentro de la estatua. Sólo en estos momentos de pérdida de conciencia, absolutamente intemporales, siento la vida, como una planta mojada que se pega a la nariz y, es táctil y fresca, en mi lengua. No poder sobrepasar esta sensación, o anular cualquier idea frente al espasmo de estar ahora, aquí, delante de mi imposibilidad humana es mi obsesión. A veces, te pones molesta y me exalto, para demostrarte que soy humana y de tu carne también.

No sé el mito que provocó estas estatuas que se acarician en perfecto triángulo. Busca otra tiza para rayar algún mito más moderno sobre el triángulo de la felicidad; para saber creer que algo no se borrará— al menos, en esta esquina, entre los leones y el mar—donde hoy jugamos a escaparnos un segundo al desastre. Ese segundo que hemos sobrevivido a la escenografía (tecnología, dólares, poder) me satisface por su eternidad. Al frente, pasan las rastras amarillas (los camellos) con trescientas personas que se atropellan por llegar a alguna parte. Yo adoro los trayectos, no el fin. Si me dispones hacia el objeto final pierdo la travesía con el asombro de no llegar, más que a lo que encontré—lo único, lo inalcanzable. Resucita con tu inocencia, rayas con tizas de colores; dibujos que antes estuvieron en las cavernas y, ahora, están con nosotras, al pie del árbol, en el centro de la fuente blanca, esta mañana, cuando decido hacerme parecida a la estatua y, verte otra vez de perfil, a través de las hojas verdes y amarillas de otros árboles que serán siempre iguales. Cuando termines de dibujar y te levantes, yo habré terminado también mi carta… y, ella—con el olor a azufre de los crematorios todavía en la piel—recibirá de este dibujo de tiza que hemos logrado hacer, el poder necesario para vencer el miedo y rescatarla y rescatarnos del horror. Sé que no es suficiente que seamos felices un instante para que ella resista, pero lo intentaremos. Lo imperecedero no es cierta metafísica, ni la creencia para sostenernos en alguna fe, sino la consecución de mí, de ti, de ella, en nosotros… La trayectoria probable de la flor—tal vez ya roja—contra el pico del pájaro, cuando vuelvas en la noche y seas otra vez, la mujer que él acariciaba.

(parque cerca del Prado)
1 de abril de 1994

VI

Llego otra vez, y recuerdo ese mismo parque que me recibió durante tantos años (el parque de la Plaza de Armas, el parque Washington, el Central Park). También recuerdo, la sensación última que tuve antes de que tú nacieras, mientras miraba las buganvillas tornasoladas —,

22

hunting birds. I know that when I go I'll end up inside the statue again. It's only in these moments of lost awareness, absolutely outside time, that I sense life, like a wet plant plastering itself to your nose, tactile, fresh on my tongue. This is my obsession: being unable to overtake this sensation or erase any idea before the spasm of being here, now, facing my human limitation. Sometimes you get annoyed and I turn emotional, in order to show you that I'm human and of your own flesh.

I don't know what myth gave rise to these statues embracing in a perfect triangle. Look for another piece of chalk to draw the lines of a more modern myth over the triangle of felicity; to know you believe that something will not blur—at least, on this corner, between lions and sea—where today we play at escaping ruination for a second. That second in which we've survived the scenario (technology, dollars, power) satisfies me in its eternity. In front, yellow crawlers (expanded buses) go by with three hundred people knocking each other over to get somewhere. I adore trajectories, not the endpoint. If you point me toward a final objective, I lose the crossing in the shock of non-arrival, anywhere but at what I've found—something unique, unattainable. With your innocence, breathe life into stripes from colored chalk; drawings that would have been in caverns in the past, and now are here with us, at the base of the tree, at the center of the white fountain, this morning, when I decide to make myself resemble the statue and see you in profile one more time, through yellow and green leaves of other trees that will always be the same. When you finish drawing and stand up, I will also have finished my letter... and she—with the sulfurous odor of crematories still on her skin—will receive from this chalk drawing we've made the power necessary to defeat fear, and to rescue her, and to rescue us from horror. I know it's not enough for us to be happy for a moment in order for her to hold out, but we'll give it a try. That which is imperishable is not a particular metaphysics, nor belief that sustains us within some faith, but the attainment of myself, of you, of her, inside us ... The probable trajectory of the flower— perhaps already red—along the bird's beak, when you might come back at night to be, again, the woman whom he was caressing.

(park next to the Prado)
1 April 1994

VI

I arrive again, and I remember the park that received me for so many years, the same one (the park at the Plaza de Armas, at Washington Park, Central Park). I also remember the last sensation I had before you were born, looking at iridescent bougainvilleas—saying goodbye.

despidiéndome. O, la suave corriente del lago y los patos salvajes o, los viejos aquellos que se sentaron junto a nosotros con un libro de la Ajmátova en ruso, ¡qué casualidad!, ver cómo ese idioma nos persigue, sin ser ya un idioma, sino un sentimiento.

Siempre son los parques los sitios donde comienzo un libro, o me despido. Ahora, fue bueno volver para escribir sobre estas cosas (porque el tiempo de la palabra sujeto a un presente absoluto, nos proporciona un futuro y un pasado absolutos, para un suceso aquí-ahora). Pero esta mañana en la que recuerdo —una tajada, una cuña en el tiempo— extraño, el compás de tu paso más corto, o el compás de su paso tan largo, mientras camino, las manos y los antebrazos están rígidos hasta dolerme, porque me acostumbré a caminar contigo. Siempre tuve un amigo con el que me acostumbré a ver las películas, otro con quien solía tomar el té, cosas muy simples en apariencia, que conforman día a día, una eternidad lograda.

Como volver contigo a la película de siempre —tal vez *Siberiada*— mientras llueve, y baja con rapidez la temperatura en N.Y. y, el cine es pequeño y está casi vacío, pero nosotros hemos rescatado del pasado, contra la lluvia fría, su dolor. Y volvemos a movernos entre dos tiempos—como entre la posibilidad y la imposibilidad de esas dos culturas, en un mismo lugar de la memoria—: cine vacío con película rusa mal traducida al inglés (no entiendo las palabras). Sólo pongo la cabeza en tu hombro y vuelvo a sentir, cómo se derriban las puertas contra el sonido, cómo se derriban las distancias, cómo chocan y caen en fragmentos... Sé que estás triste, ya ves, a veces nos despedimos de las personas que más queremos. Pero donde yo esté, tú estarás. Porque creo en un paisaje que se traslada desde los objetos, los edificios, las plantas y las personas, hasta moverse sobre superficies paralelas (virtuales, continuas) que van con uno a todas partes.

Extrañas, porque extraño. Recoges los objetos caídos con los pies en forma de tijeras—como yo—, me repites, me rompes. Eres la niña con el ramo de flores moradas y la bata con el reflejo lila. Estás en el columpio conmigo. El hombre de traje y boina rusa está a mi lado y vemos *Siberiada*, una película tan ajena y tan nuestra. No volveremos a ser nuestro pasado, no volveremos a intentarlo, pero aún, se nos permite recordar, a pesar de la indiferencia y el cansancio de los otros.

Dormimos en la casita y la noche nos traga—otra noche doméstica en este cine mental—con la negrura dentro de su boca tan roja. Relampaguea, llueve, suenan las gotas sobre el techo, más fuertes, más rápidas—te protejo de tu miedo y del mío, con ese goce perfecto de ser uno y otro, a la vez.

Or, the smooth current of the lake and wild ducks, or those old men who sat down next to us with a book by Akhmatova in Russian, what a coincidence!, seeing how that language pursues us without existing as a language anymore; instead it's a feeling.

Parks are always the places where I begin a book or say goodbye. Now it was good to return and write about these things (because the time of the word subjected to an absolute present supplies us with an absolute future and past, for an event in the here and now). But this morning when I remember—a slice, a wedge in time—while out walking, I feel nostalgia for the measure of your step, shorter, or the measure of her step, so long, my hands and forearms so rigid they hurt, because I got used to walking with you. I always had one friend with whom I watched movies, another with whom I drank tea. Things very simple in appearance comprising, one day after another, the achievement of eternity.

Like going back with you to the usual movie—perhaps *Siberiade*—while it rains, and the temperature drops rapidly in N.Y., and the theater is small and nearly empty, but we've rescued its pain from the past, against a chilly rainfall. And we move again between two points in time—as between the possibility and impossibility of those two cultures, remembered in the same place: empty theater, Russian film badly translated into English (I don't understand the words). I just put my head on your shoulder and feel how the doors knock against sound again, how distances knock together, how they crash and fall in fragments... I know you're sad, you see, sometimes we say goodbye to the people we love the most. But wherever I may be, you'll be. Because I believe in a traveling landscape: from its objects, buildings, plants and people, down to its motion over parallel surfaces (virtual, constant), which go along with us everywhere.

You're homesick because I'm homesick. You pick up fallen objects by scissoring your feet—like me—you repeat me, you break me. You're the girl with a sprig of purple flowers and the coat reflecting lilac. You're on the swing with me. The man in a jacket and Russian beret is at my side and we're watching *Siberiade*, a film that is so alien and so much ours. We won't go back to be our past again, we won't try to do it over, but we're allowed to remember in spite of the others, their indifference and exhaustion.

In the little house we sleep and night swallows us—another domestic night in this mental cinema—with the blackness inside her mouth, so red. Lightning, rain, drops smack against the roof, harder, quicker—I protect you from your fear, and from mine, with that perfect enjoyment of being one and other at the same time.

VII

Uno cría a una muchacha para que se haga otro (esa mujer) y también cría a un hombre con uno—el hombre siempre está ahí para matarla—: él, la persigue desde niña. Es un monstruo, es su padre, un gato, o un ángel bellísimo. (Tal vez preferiría que fuera un elefante.) La custodia y la espera al final para desflorarla. Ese rostro que se borra con la niebla de los acontecimientos y que una luz opaca ilumina al final, es el rostro que andas buscando. Nunca lo encontrarás. Es hombre, mujer y niño—pájaro. También es gato y avestruz. Pero casi nunca logra ser un elefante. Él llega a perseguirte en los momentos de mayor vacío (también puede ser mujer). Es blanco y de ojos azules (como en la novela de Margaritte Duras)... Es Ismael (el de *Fanny y Alexander*). Por esos ojos dentro de mí, yo sé que tengo un corazón. Él también lo sabe y te persigue, para que tu corazón—y el suyo—, que puede ser un reloj sin esfera, no deje de latir (el tiempo absoluto que es ahora, la zona neutral en forma de cuña, de su reloj de arena).

Estoy en la manicura Milena, ya que no quiero estar en ninguna parte, o decidir, entré a este sin lugar que para nada me interesa, pensando en cambiar, o dejar algo: arrancarme las uñas, cortarme el pelo al rente. Pero me falta valor para ser otra (mis narraciones se dispersan sin la fuerza sólo para crear un triángulo y su filosofía). Yo también necesito dos hombres, y busco a hombres que necesiten a su vez, al suyo. Sólo así me equilibro en el triángulo de la muerte. Estando uno en mi mente y otro a mis pies, no me ahogo en el ojo absoluto del mar. Esa sería una irreparable pérdida: la entrega. (Como abuela fabricó con dos fotos de primos muertos al tío ficticio, yo fabrico mis hombres a semejanza y opuesto al perseguidor.)

No soporto la mecánica de ese animal que enrojece—no por contacto—sino por estímulos históricos que han reducido su creación al vacío. Cuando un hombre se acuclilla frente a ti, comprendes con decepción, que él no halló la variación necesaria para hallar lo distinto y se conformó con la reiteración. Una especie reiterativa y mecánica por miles de años, por eso se extinguió. Algunos salpican como regaderas. Otros se espesan hasta formar su dibujo, manchándote.

No te voy a dar recetas. Pero, entre esas acrobacias de la especie para provocar una manera de sentir (de fin o de resurrección) y el verdadero goce, está la distancia del Don. El Don está en la sangre y te hace vibrar por otros cruces que no tienen cabezas. El Don no usa las posturas del hábito y planea sin él. No te acostumbres a recibir por el camino de siempre. Cada uno (que es un niño y una muchacha y un muchacho también) sabrá de gestos que lo conduzcan a uno mismo.

VII

You raise a girl in order to become other (that woman) and also bring up a man alongside your own self—the man is always there to kill her—: he, he pursues her from childhood onward. He's a monster, he's her father, a cat, or a beautiful angel. (Maybe he'd prefer to be an elephant.) He protects her and waits at the end to deflower her. That face, it's erased by the fog of events, lit with an opaque light at the end, the face you seek. You'll never find it. The face is man, woman, and child—bird. Cat and ostrich too. But it almost never gets to be an elephant. He comes to pursue you in your moments of great emptiness (can exist as a woman too). White, blue-eyed (like in the novel by Marguerite Duras)... he's Ismael (the one from Fanny and Alexander). Thanks to those eyes inside myself, I know I have a heart. He knows it too and pursues you, so your heart—and his—which may be a clock with no face—won't stop ticking (absolute time: the now, the neutral zone in the wedge of an hourglass).

I'm at the manicurist, Milena, since I don't want to be anywhere or make a decision, I came into this completely uninteresting nonplace, I was thinking about how to change or get rid of something: pull out my nails, cut off all my hair. But I lack the courage to be someone else (my stories disperse without enough strength to create a triangle and its philosophy). Like her I need two men, and I look for men who might in turn need theirs. Only in this way can I balance on death's triangle. One in my mind, the other at my feet, I won't drown in the absolute eye of the ocean. That would be an irreparable loss: the surrender. (As when my grandmother fabricated a fictitious uncle out of two photos of dead cousins, I fabricate my men in resemblance and opposition to the pursuer).

I can't stand the mechanics of the animal that flushes red—not from contact but from historical stimuli, which have reduced its creation to a vacuum. When a man squats before you, you understand, disappointed, that he couldn't find necessary variations for meeting with difference, so he settled for repetition. A repetitive species, mechanical for thousands of years, that's why it went extinct. Some send out spatters like showerheads. Others thicken into a drawing, leaving you with stains.

I won't give you prescriptions. But between these acrobatic moves by the species, meant to provoke some way of feeling (end or resurrection) and true pleasure, you find the distance of the Gift. The Gift comes down through the blood and makes you quiver even though you have no knowledge of its path. The Gift does not adopt customary views. It makes its plans without them. Don't get used to receiving things in the same old way. Every person (a child, a girl, and a boy too) will learn from gestures that point him toward himself.

(Así Wang-Fu amaba la imagen de las cosas y no las cosas en sí mismas.) Abre los ojos y lávate la cara. Mira cuanto puedas los labios y los dientes que yo no miré y esa belleza será también tuya, por opuesto y semejanza. No trates de fundir al hombre mental (al perseguidor) con el real. Ellos tienen cada uno su lugar y en la utopía de realizarlos se va el tiempo del presente. Así gasté mis noches y mis días, esperándolo…

Lo que sugiere que la cuña neutral se podría llamar presente-absoluto. Desde esta perspectiva, la característica del ahora en un suceso que más lejos extenderá la sombra de su umbra.

VIII

Querida Elis Milena, no sólo se empequeñeció y se redujo la intensidad de la luz y del espacio como si hubiera sido colada hacia la parte más estrecha del túnel, más bien, del embudo. Empecé a dar, y a reducirme. Durante los primeros quince días el tiempo se dilató—parecía que hubieran pasado largos años—, y la fábula sustituyó, para tantos oídos deseantes, toda la capacidad de acción. Fui vaciándome de peso, de zapatos, de jabones, hasta que no tenía ya nada que dar ni qué contar… Y "el viaje", pasó a ser una región de color en el espacio de mi cabeza que intentaba todavía poseer y, a la vez, entregar cosas imposibles. Empezó la angustia por las pequeñas cosas de la supervivencia—esa rusticidad de lo perentorio—y también, la dinámica de mi libertad se redujo a lo mínimo. Como si el regreso sucediera en otro tiempo, con otra velocidad. Todos tiranizan tu espacio de recuerdo, lo observan y finalmente, lo aniquilan.

Yo había cruzado dispuesta a que no me lo quitaran. Veía con claridad los despilfarros de los eventos inútiles en los que malgastamos el placer. Esos comentarios, los gestos, la siniestra piratería y hasta la mezquindad otorgados por la inercia y el desencanto. El desastre mayor no era sólo económico, sino sicológico.

Mis amigos (los más inteligentes) habían apostado sus vidas a la observación a través de un microscopio vulgar, bajo el cual hacían mínimas evoluciones por debajo de su capacidad para sobrevivir. El grado de esquizofrenia (aquí—y también allá—, del otro lado del túnel, era bien contagioso). Todos llegaban tarde al reparto de las actuaciones y entraban desnudos en el set. Y surgió en mí la conciencia de este horror, el vértigo de su retórica. Allí donde no quedaba nada ya que sostener, como en "Sin" o "El despoblador", de Beckett; allí, donde las zonas de posibilidad se obstruían, o cortaban sin nacer aún—o vencer—, sustituían a la razón ciertas lógicas de resolver a toda costa lo inmediato,

(This is how Wang Fu loved the image of things and not the things in themselves.) Open your eyes and wash your face. Look as long as you can at your lips and teeth, as I did not, and that beauty will be yours through opposition and resemblance. Don't try to merge the mental man (the pursuer) into the real one. Each has his own place, and in the utopia of their realization, time runs out for the present. I used up my nights and days like that, waiting for him…

Which suggests the neutral wedge could be called present-absolute. From this perspective: the characteristic of the now, in an event that will further extend the shade from its shadow.

VIII

Dear Elis Milena, it wasn't only that the intensity of light and space shrank and dwindled, as if it had drained off toward the narrowest section of the tunnel, or better said, the funnel. I began to give of myself and dwindle. During the first fifteen days, time dilated—it seemed that long years must have passed—and to so many desiring ears, the fabula substituted for all capacity to act. I was dropping weight, getting rid of shoes, soaps, until I had nothing left to give away or recount… And "the journey" came to be a region in color, a mental space I still attempted to possess while simultaneously surrendering impossible things. The anguish came with little details of survival—the crudeness of urgency—and the dynamics of my freedom shrank to a minimum. As if the return were occurring in a different time, with a different velocity. Everyone oppresses the space you have for memories; they observe it, and then they destroy it.

I had crossed over with the attitude that they wouldn't take it away from me. I could clearly see the waste from futile events, as we misused pleasure. Those commentaries, the gestures, the catastrophic piracy and even nastiness produced by inertia and disillusionment. The greatest disaster wasn't merely economic, but psychological.

My friends (the most intelligent ones) had wagered their lives under observation through a vulgar microscope, where they made minimal evolutions through their capacity to survive. The degree of schizophrenia (here—and also there—on the other side of the tunnel, it was quite contagious). Everyone got there late when the parts were being handed out; we walked onto the set naked. And inside me an awareness of horror grew, vertigo from their rhetoric. There where nothing was left to sustain, like in Beckett's "Lessness" or "The Lost Ones"; there, where the zones of possibility were becoming blocked, or cut off before any birth—or victory—in place of reason they substituted certain logics for getting through the short

por lo que el camino más fácil era la fuga, un "no sé", la indiferencia. También es imposible salirse del redil. Te castra esa mayoría que respira alargando la nariz contra tu respiración. Te ahoga quien pretendiendo salvarte se coloca tras tu cuello, dentro de esa masa de inválidos amorfos desesperados por llegar a otra orilla rodeada de gases sulfurosos. Entonces, aparecen vestigios sórdidos de la personalidad y del ego robustecidos en la lucha por adquirir un lugar que no existe para ellos.

Tuve entonces que adaptarme y aceptar la paranoia que me rodeaba como algo normal, adquirida por la circunstancia de no ser normales, así como otros subterfugios que dilapidaban mi energía. No sólo había perdido el centro, sino la visión que me permitía relacionar a cierta distancia, con intervalos de comprensión profundos, la llama.

La frecuencia sobre la que montamos las imágenes son hiperrealistas y destruyen su erótica, por la realidad. Comprendí, que el problema de salir (me refiero a cualquier tipo de salida o búsqueda) no es constatar, o medir, a través de una comparación elemental, qué somos, que hemos hecho con nuestra existencia. Es comprender que se ha producido una cerebración para la cual no hay lugar estético. Que no hay todavía una estética—que como una filiación profunda, de amistad, o de amor—relacione lo concebido con su inmediata materialización. Esa falta de coordinación agranda el sentimiento de relatividad y de culpa, confundiéndonos más.

Ahora estoy indiferente al dolor que me provoca esta comprensión. Tengo un acomodo frío y hasta impersonal que me despoja—no de las acciones con las que no cuento ya para mí, todo sucede—, sino de una pasión absurda por su materialización en el aquí-ahora. ¿Qué puedo hacer entonces? Como un malogrado actor, trato de establecer los espacios de mis gestos sin acortarlos, sin condicionarlos, manteniéndolos vivos para su pequeña intensidad (inconclusa). Coloco el carrusel de mis seres discontinuos en un acomodo verbal, para salirme de una estructura que me hace subsidiarlos y hacerlos dependientes. Entonces allí, algo más libre—en la aparente indiferencia a esa razón que los posesiona (y, a pesar de mi constante complejo de culpa)—, amarlos, sin pretender que me comprendan.

Sé que te he escrito esta carta con zonas del lenguaje que no comprenderás. Pero creo, como aquellos ciegos de la fábula del elefante, que con tu mano sobre la escritura derritiéndola, sentirás la emoción única de las letras dentro de las cuales quise simplificar esta agonía, quise decir: ¡qué ha pasado aquí! ¿Qué ha pasado aquí?

En cualquier parte de este planeta donde se viva es ridículo

term at all costs, through which the easiest route was escape, an "I dunno," indifference. It was also impossible to exit the fold. They neuter you, the majority who breathe by stretching their noses into your breath. They drown you, the ones who try to save you by getting behind your neck, in that mass of amorphous invalids desperate to arrive at the other shore in a cloud of sulfuric gases. Then sordid traces of personality and ego appear, strengthened in the fight to get a place that doesn't exist for them.

At that point I had to adapt and accept the paranoia surrounding me as something normal, acquired in the circumstances of not being normal, like other subterfuges that squandered my energy. I hadn't only lost the center, but the vision—the one that used to allow me to relate from a certain distance, with intervals of deep understanding, the flame.

The speed with which we assemble images, they're hyper-realist and destroy erotics through reality. I came to understand that the problem of departing (I refer to any type of departure or search) is not constituted, or measured, through an elemental comparison—the what are we?, what have we done with our existence. It's understanding that a cerebration has been produced for which there is no aesthetic place. That there is still no aesthetic which, like a profound filiation, of friendship or love, could relate the thing conceived to its immediate materialization. That lack of coordination extends the feeling of relativity and guilt, confusing us more.

Now I'm indifferent to the pain that provokes my understanding. I allow for it, coldly and so impersonally that it strips me—not of the actions on which I no longer count for myself, everything happens—but of an absurd passion for its materialization in the here and now. So what can I do? Like a failed actor, I try to establish spaces for my gestures without constricting them, without making them conditional, keeping them alive for their small (incomplete) form of intensity. I place the carousel of my discontinuous selves into a verbal form of allowance, to get out of a structure that forces me to subsidize them, make them dependent. So there, a bit more free—apparently indifferent to the reason that takes possession of them (in spite of my continual guilt complex)—loving them, without trying to make them understand me.

I know I've written you this letter in regions of language you won't understand. But I think that like those blind men from the elephant fable, when you put your hand onto the writing, thawing it, you'll sense the unique emotion of the writing, inside which I tried to simplify this agony, tried to say: what has happened here! what has happened here?

Wherever one lives on this planet it's ridiculous to try to escape. I refer only to figures that make up certain more subtle forms of logic, which

pretender escapar. Sólo me refiero a las figuras que conforman ciertas lógicas más sutiles que deconstruyen al hombre en acciones concretas contra su cuerpo, o su alma. Hablo, Elis, de las fisuras por las que—lo que Milena sintió en el campo durante los trabajos forzados y el olor a carne quemada de los crematorios—, están también en mí, en ti, y nos acechan.

Las figuras de esta geometría del infierno con ampollas virulentas cuyo dolor ya hizo metástasis, darán después su contrapartida en lenguaje.

Sé que este delirio del que te hablo y no puedes aún calcular, no es para ti. Y, no sé si me podrás perdonar este descuido por hacer un dibujo consciente. Quisiera volver al garabato, a la contemplación, pero a veces, no se pueden desmontar tantas cosas. ¡He montado y desmontado tantas cosas! Que no sé. Son como puñetazos de una vejez prematura con los que uno pretende sintetizar (o cuantificar) los resultados. ¿De qué?, nunca se sabe o se sospecha bien, de qué. Son esos pináculos o torcimientos del paisaje que obstruyen el lenguaje y dificultan que en algunos momentos, tú estés completamente en mí, que uno esté, donde debería únicamente estar, completamente en todo.

Siguen cayéndose los edificios y del otro lado de las fachadas, ese todo me ha demostrado con más fuerza, el alcance de mi irrealidad y la fisura misma de lo simbólico. Es necesario deshacer nuestro real bajo el efecto de otras escenas y otra sintaxis. Tal vez rehacerlas con lo más simple... con lo que quedó.

IX

La luz de Madrid es más plomiza, encapotada, sobre las plazas arenosas donde cocean los caballos. Las aceras son más anchas y las palomas bajan desde todos los ángulos y parten al menor roce. El Metro Arguelles-Lavapies me recuerda a aquel de Palo Verde a Propatria, en Caracas. Estás en Europa y en América a la vez. Las calles no son indiferentes, o extrañas. Hay algo familiar en ese humor íntimo que se acerca a las cosas. Pensé en ti, en la calle de Alcalá y en la Gran Vía. Quería llevarte una manta de allí, pero eran muy caras. Pasé del frío al calor de la mañana de plaza de plaza. Intenté entrar muy temprano a una iglesia pero, curiosamente, abren muy tarde. Vi los Boteros del Retiro y los toqué. Toqué sus nalgas ampulosas, sus formas deformadas. Cuatro días bajando y subiendo por las plazas, las esculturas, los museos, las tabernas, me despertaron a una conciencia erótica de la ciudad, donde el objeto humano o no, no era indispensable para el hallazgo de esa sensación, pues giraba dentro de ella, entraba por las cañerías, por los edificios, bajo los adoquines, dentro de mi camita de flores en el hostal,

deconstruct man through concrete actions against his body, or his soul. I'm speaking, Elis, about the fissure through which—what Milena sensed in the camp during forced labor, the smell of burnt flesh from the crematories— they're inside me too, and you, and they're lying in wait for us.

The figures of this hellish geometry, with virulent blisters whose pain has already metastasized. They'll give compensation later in language.

I know this delirium I'm telling you about, one with which you can't yet reckon, is not for you. And I don't know if you'll be able to forgive me for this lapse of so consciously laying out a drawing. I've tried to go back to my scribble, to contemplation, but sometimes, there are so many things that can't be dismantled. I've assembled and dismantled so many things! that I don't know. They're like blows from premature aging, out of which one tries to synthesize (or quantify) results. For what? One never knows or suspects with any clarity. They're those pinnacles or twists in the landscape that block language and make it difficult for you, in some moments, to be completely inside of me, for one to be, wherever one in particular ought to be, completely inside the whole.

The buildings keep falling down and from the other side of the facades, the whole has shown me, with greater force, the reach of my unreality, the fissure from that which is symbolic. We have to unmake our reality under the influence of other scenes and another syntax. Maybe to remake them with the simplest thing... with what remained.

IX

Light in Madrid is more the color of lead, cloudy, cast over sandy plazas where horses kick. The sidewalks are wider and the pigeons descend from all angles, flying off at the slightest contact. The subway stop at Arguelles-Lavapies reminds me of one in Caracas, the Palo Verde at Propatria. You're in Europe and America at the same time. The streets aren't indifferent or strange. There's something familiar about the intimate humor brought to things. I thought about you on the Calle de Alcalá and the Gran Vía. I wanted to bring a blanket back for you, but they were too expensive. I moved from plaza to plaza, from the morning's cold to warmth. I tried to get into a church early in the morning but they open strangely late. I saw the Boteros at Retiro Park and touched them. I touched their bombastic asses, their deformed forms. Four days of walking up and down through the plazas, sculptures, museums, taverns, awoke in me an erotic awareness of the city, where the object, human or otherwise, was not essential for finding that sensation, since I rotated through it, got in through the pipes, the buildings, under the paving stones, inside my little flowery bed

por los espejos de los almacenes, por los zapatos de moda con corchos por suelas, la tela coloreada, ¡mi alegría! ¡Me gustaría tanto traerte aquí! Y recordé tus bailes españoles en la azotea, tu Tani. Tu cara de niña prometiendo una maja. La foto de la niña que fui, con el traje de óvalos rojos y las argollas de plata de la infancia. Las castañuelas de granadina tan pequeñas que se podían esconder dentro de las manos. Un sonido agazapado, pero constante. Una ilusión de ser, como la Macarena, la réplica de esa virgen del cuadro.

También vi una película, *El piano*, y te recordé. Una mujer que ha enmudecido da un viaje con su hija (de tu misma edad) para casarse. La película transcurre en el sigo XVII. El sonido del piano (aun sin tocar), lo lleva en su cabeza, cuando toca en las maderas de la cocina, de los árboles, de las entrañas con sus nudillos, hasta que consigue materializar su música por todas partes. El marido—por aquella infidelidad de poseer un don que al acercarla al piano, la ha acercado también a otro hombre—le corta los dedos de un hachazo.

"Pues entonces es el fin—le dice Kafka a Milena—y es casi imposible describir cómo se las arregla uno para salvarse..."

De regreso de ese viaje malogrado, ella intenta hundirse con su piano en el mar, y sale desde fondo del océano para aceptar la realidad, su medianía, su mediocridad: un dedo de metal, una escuela donde impartirá clases a las señoritas y donde aprenderá a hablar—como todos los demás—sin música.

Para ser aceptados hay que pactar con cierta medianía. (Yo también lo hice, hija mía.) He tocado sobre muchas cosas absurdas, inmerecidas, mi dedo de metal.

Todavía sé que sueñas con "tu varita mágica". Siempre me has dicho que tu secreto es poseer esa varita para resolver cosas imposibles de la realidad. Algún día, seguro, la tendrás.

La protagonista se parece a mí—en la visión ingrata de un espejo—, y la niña, a ti. Salí del cine descompuesta. Lloré. Lo único que quería era volver y abrazarte.

Aterrizamos bien...

En el aeropuerto, empieza la cola y la amargura. El calor y esas luces bajitas, de una ciudad tan amada que no se puede perder, ni conquistar. Cuando grité desde la calle para que ustedes bajaran a recoger las maletas, ¡los vi a todos tan frágiles! Cómo se habían reducido el espacio y la luz, también sus cuerpos se habían reducido en poco tiempo. Y sentí de nuevo un empequeñecimiento de la visión, como si me hubiera trasladado a un pueblito de postal en otra época.

in the cheap hotel, through the department store mirrors, through the trendy cork-soled shoes, the colorful fabric, my darling! I'd like so much to bring you here! And I remembered your Spanish dances at home on the roof, your Tani. Your little-girl face with its promise of a *maja*. The photo of the little girl I once was, in a red polka-dot suit and a child's silver bracelets. Grenadine castanets tiny enough to be hidden inside one's hands. A sound poised yet constant. An illusion of being, like the Virgen de la Macarena, a replica of the virgin in the painting.

I also saw a film, *The Piano*, and remembered you. A woman who has lost her voice travels with her daughter (your exact age) to get married. The film takes place in the nineteenth century. She carries the sound of the piano (still without playing it) in her mind, when she touches the wooden countertops, the trees, the entrails with her knuckles, until she manages to make her music present in all places. The husband—because of her infidelity in having a gift that brings her close not only to the piano, but to another man—cuts off her fingers with an axe.

"Well then it's the end"—Kafka says to Milena—and it's almost impossible to describe how one manages to survive…"

Upon return from that ill-fated trip, she tries to drown herself with her piano in the ocean, then leaves the ocean floor to accept reality, her average state, her mediocrity: a metal finger, a school where she will teach classes to young ladies and learn how to speak—like all the others—without music.

To be accepted, one must compromise with a certain mediocrity. (I did it doo, my daughter.) I've run my metal finger over many absurd, undeserved things.

I know you still dream of "your magic wand." You've always told me that your secret is having a wand for resolving the impossible parts of reality. Someday, I'm sure, you'll have it.

The protagonist resembles me—through a mirror's unpleasant reflection—and the girl you. I left the theater without composure. I cried. The only thing I wanted was to go back and hug you.

We land safely…

In the airport, the lines and the bitterness start up. The heat and those low lights, from a city so beloved that it can't be lost or conquered. When I shouted up from the street so you would all come down to help with suitcases, everyone looked so fragile! As if space and light had shrunk, and your bodies too, in that short time. And once again I felt a shrinking of my vision, as if I were transported to a pueblo in a postcard from another era.

Estaba otra vez aquí, contigo—desde donde intento, alternando la relatividad imposible de los tiempos verbales—, contarte mi viaje. Tú habías llorado varias veces. Yo nunca te olvidé (ese temor de olvidar me hace volver rápidamente y rescatar la fijeza). Pero sobre todo, comprendí que el momento no está dado por las tangentes que provocamos, o usamos, para acortar la distancia y el miedo. Que el momento sucede, sin nuestra intervención. El momento es una decisión íntima de la materia acumulada. Llega y sucede cuando es.

La fragilidad de la mayoría consiste en violentar ese espacio, persiguiéndolo. No adelantar nada, no preparar algo, o el camino se llena de cruces advenedizas, también en la realidad de la página. El momento es de una capacidad erótica que sobrepasa a las intenciones, los gestos, las interpretaciones, incluso, nuestras intuiciones. La persona que uno es (y que uno era), está concebida—como previamente editada—para su escena permanente. Tampoco se puede escoger—él, lo elige a uno—, y lo coloca en la situación de advenedizo que todavía se cree, o sueña creer, con la confianza de querer, hacer, y poseer.

Espero que algún día comprendas estas cosas y que podamos hacer la travesía juntas, para que bailes... "Por las calles de Alcalá".

La Habana, junio de 1994

X

Nunca supe qué tipo de relación se estableció entre Kafka y Milena. Hacía muchos años que no leía sus cartas. Elis Milena (la mía); Milena (tú, la del campo de concentración, la suya). Mi hija nació el 3 de julio como Kafka. Su primer nombre hubiera sido Milena, por él. Pero no quería romper la antigua tradición de mi familia, su preferencia por las E. En fin, cuando empecé la primera carta en el aeropuerto, el día que se fue el avión para Viena con el equipaje y sin mí, pensé en ese nombre como síntesis de muchos acontecimientos que nos unían. Había leído una biografía de Milena y tenía en el librero, justo frente a mi cama, su fotografía. No quería para ti, ni para ella, aquel destino. Sentía, no obstante, esa relación en un tiempo de "lo real" pervertido siempre por algún sueño de poder. Busqué, entonces, otras cartas. Leí las de madame de Sevigné, a su hija. Yo no estaba en la corte entre príncipes, ni hablaríamos de tus próximos peinados, pero siempre hay una corte alrededor de una mujer aunque no exista, aquí, la monarquía. En ese trayecto de romper un viaje para emprender otro, de proporciones diferentes, hallé ese tiempo de la niña perdida, asombrada también de ver con los mismos ojos y dentro del desastre, la flor que

I was here again, with you—from where I try, alternating the impossible relativity of verbal tempos—to tell you all about my trip. You had cried many times. I never forgot you (that fear of forgetting makes me return quickly and retrieve constancy). But above all I realized that the moment is not given through the tangents we may provoke, or use, to cut back the distance and the fear. Let the moment happen without our intervention. The moment is an intimate decision of accumulated material. It arrives and happens when it is.

The frailty of the majority consists of its assault on space, hunting it down. Not moving anything forward or preparing anything, or the road fills with foreign crossroads, also on the reality of the page. The moment is an erotic capacity that exceeds intentions, gestures, interpretations, even our intuitions. The person whom you are (and were) is conceived—as previously edited—for her permanent scene. Nor can you choose—him, he chooses—to place yourself in the situation of foreignness that you still believe, or dream of believing, with the confidence of desiring, making, and possessing.

I hope that one day you'll understand these things and we can make the crossing together, so you will dance… "through the streets of Alcalá."

Havana, June 1994

X

I never figured out what kind of relationship there was between Kafka and Milena. For many years I hadn't read his letters. Elis Milena (my Milena); Milena (you, the concentration camp Milena, his Milena). My daughter was born on July 3, like Kafka. Her first name would have been Milena, through him. But I didn't want to break my family's long tradition, its preference for the letter E. In the end, when I began the first letter at the airport, the day the plane went off to Vienna with my luggage but not me, I thought about that name as the synthesis of many occurrences connecting us. I had read a biography of Milena and had her photograph on the bookshelf, right by my bed. I didn't want that destiny for you or her. All the same I sensed the relation in a time when "the real" is always perverted by some dream of power. Then I went looking for other letters. I read the ones from Madame de Sevigne to her daughter. I was not at court among princes, and we wouldn't talk about your next hairstyle, but there's always a court surrounding a woman even if monarchy doesn't exist here. Along that trajectory of breaking off one journey in order to undertake another one of different proportions, I found time for the lost girl, who is also surprised, who from the inside of disaster regards the

empieza a crecer incluso, a pesar suyo. Esa eres tú, mi pequeña Elis, la que empieza a crecer dentro del desastre.

Todos sentimos una atracción morbosa por el terror y, a la vez, todo terror, nos consume en una semejanza paralela, aunque sus manifestaciones externas sean o parezcan, diferentes.

Eso he sentido, mientras muchas personas se echan al mar, enloquecidas ante la muerte rotunda de un "lo mismo da", o durante la espera de una vida soñada.

Para ese abuso del destino, yo interpuse el refugio de la palabra en la construcción de espacios de relación, entre la madre que fui y la hija que seré. Si reitero ese instante, es porque me da la posibilidad de construir un dibujo que confina al sujeto a un por qué. Todo es anterior y después.

El día que termino el libro, comienzo a empezarlo. Con tu nacimiento, Milena, vuelve a sobrevivir. Nada de esto es casual. No optamos. Sólo inclinamos un poco más el reencuentro con alguna posición en el espacio y en el tiempo.

Hay una reversibilidad del tiempo biológico en la cultura, por lo que el futuro determina al presente mucho más que el pasado. Es cierto—dicen los científicos—que la entropía de un sistema abierto disminuye. No sé nada de ciencias exactas, sólo intuyo el sistema abierto a la creación y esa movilidad del tiempo en múltiples direcciones. Miro Autorretrato con reloj de pared, de Chagall y tomo en cuenta la distracción, el ruido y el azar. Tus ojos son color alita de cucaracha (otra relación kafkiana). Agrupé los dibujos. Quería aconsejarte sobre algo y desistí. ¿Aconsejarte o mentirte sobre qué? Dejé entonces todo lo recopilado y preferí deletrear lo que en mi cerebración iba formándose en el aquí-ahora. Surgió a la misma distancia del ojo del gato que me está contemplando, un género que aún no puedo comprender, al que tal vez, llegaré. El gato me ha entendido.

Hay sólo una energía mal traducida por las palabras, corregida luego por la pulsión de la máquina. Por eso, primero escribí a mano con letra pequeñísima, para ajustar más el viaje de la cabeza al papel, si esto no es una trampa también.

Pero Milena está aquí (como Katherine, Silvia, Simonne, Virginia y tantas otras). Porque el proceso incesante de insertar está más determinado por lo que ocurrirá que por lo que ya ha ocurrido. El futuro rige, arregla y mejora, el boceto. Y esta inversión en la individualidad es el resultado, no de una voluntad consciente (ni de la voluntad de dios domada en este sentido), sino de una mezcla entre un programa,

flower with the same eyes, the one that begins to grow even to its sorrow. That flower is you, my tiny Elis, one who begins to grow inside disaster.

We all feel a morbid attraction to terror and at the same time, all terror consumes us in a parallel likeness, though its external manifestations may be, or seem, different.

That's what I've felt, while many people throw themselves into the sea, crazed by the flat death in which "it doesn't matter," or in the long wait for a life they dreamed.

For that abuse of fate, I interjected refuge from the word into the construction of spaces of relation, relation between the mother I once was and the daughter I'll be. If I repeat that instant, it's because it gives me the possibility of constructing a sketch that confines the subject to a question of why. Everything is prior and subsequent.

The day I finish the book, I start to begin it. With your birth, Milena, it comes back to life. Nothing about this comes by chance. We don't choose. We just tilt the re-encounter a little more toward a particular position in space and time.

There's a reversability to biological time in culture, in which the future determines the present much more than the past does. It's true—scientists say—that the entropy in an open system diminishes. I know nothing of exact sciences, just intuit the system open to creation and time's mobility in multiple directions. I look at Self-portrait with Clock, by Chagall, and take the distraction, noise and chance into account. Your eyes are the color of a cockroach wing (another relation to Kafka). I grouped the drawings. I wanted to give you advice about something but held off. Give you advice or lie to you about what? So I set aside everything I had compiled and instead prioritized the spelling out of the thing taking shape in the here and now, in my cerebration. It appeared as far away as the eye of the cat looking at me, a genre I still can't comprehend, at which maybe I'll arrive. The cat understands me.

There's only a form of energy badly translated by the words, then corrected by the keyboard's drive. So first I wrote by hand in very small lettering, the better to adjust the mind's voyage to the paper, if that's not a trap as well.

But Milena is here (like Katherine, Sylvia, Simone, Virginia and so many others). Because the incessant process of insertion is determined more by what will happen than what has already happened. The future prevails, arranges and improves the model. And this investment in individuality is the result not of a conscious will (nor the will of god guided in this sense) but a mixture between a program, undetermined

los actos no determinados y la naturaleza. Creo también, porque tú existes, que el paso del tiempo siempre es creativo, nunca—a pesar de los actos de la superficie que quieren demostrar lo contrario—destructor.

Mientras el reloj del cuadro de Chagall se mece con su péndulo amarillo en la pared (los lugares de poder son amarillos—dicen) y la niña azul sobre el cuadro naranja, sueña que volvió de aquel antes, volando. Y en ese después de su infancia sostenida, rumia el proceso de crecer, con una intención doble sobre la franja del tiempo absoluta.

Ánimas, 20 de julio 1994

XI

En tus dibujos se conjugan tres elementos: la persona, la casa y la naturaleza. Como yo, ya estás haciendo el triángulo. Con este libro de cartas para ti y para esa niña que fui, he querido armar también un triángulo. La madre que seré, la hija que fui, más la escritora que he pretendido ser. No es que me impaciente algún sentido de la trascendencia (el olvido al que aspiro, así como el recuerdo que necesito, no llegarán por ahí). Sólo quiero contemplarte bajo este aire del verano que aparece con intermitencia, aunque hoy estemos prisioneras de las circunstancias. Quiero la reproducción, esa danza dentro del cuadro de Chagall, sus murmullos, para vencer el horror de este destino y las barreras de la mediocridad, que es la peor de las enfermedades humanas. Quiero la fiesta, el apogeo de su vuelo para ti. Estoy emotiva y ridícula.

En la calle, un ruido sordo de máquina perforadora para abrir la tierra tortura mis sentidos. Todo acontece así, entre un propósito ideal y la realidad roturándonos. Nada imaginamos sobre esta perfección que llegue a anular la dualidad. Detén los relojes mecánicos para "donner le change"—dice él—desde la pared. Dar el cambio, dar el pego. Siempre a través de una operación de los sentidos que nunca es mecánica.

Pensé hacerte una carta sobre la indiferencia, otra sobre la razón, algunas sobre las mujeres célebres (Anaïs, Virginia, Clarisse, la baronesa de Blixen, Djuna Barnes, como la gata fea). Pero comprendí que no era necesario. Tú buscarás a tus amigas muertas del destino (del destierro), y la historia de aquella Milena que descendió a los infiernos de un campo de concentración nazi. Ser libre es vencer la osadía de ser mujer. Traerla para un presente absoluto, aquí-ahora.

Está allí, en su postal, enviada desde Alemania por un desconocido, fija en la noche, con una tachuela al librero. Sus ojos claros y serenos que no han demostrado—sólo agua profunda y transparente

acts, and nature. I think too, because you exist, that the passage of time is always creative, never—in spite of superficial acts that seek to demonstrate the contrary—destructive.

While the clock in Chagall's painting rocks with its yellow pendulum on the wall (places of power are yellow, they say) and the blue girl on the orange canvas dreams that she returned from that earlier time, flying. And in that time after her extended childhood, she ruminates on the process of growing, intention doubled, over the wrinkle in absolute time.

Ánimas, 20 July 1994

XI

Three elements converge in your drawings: person, house, and nature. Like me, you're already working in triangles. With this book of letters for you, and for the girl I once was, I've tried to establish another triangle. The mother I will be and the daughter I used to be, plus the writer I've attempted to be. It's not that any sense of transcendence exasperates me (the oblivion to which I aspire, like the memory I need—neither one will get anywhere). I just want to contemplate you through this intermittent summer breeze, even though today we may be prisoners of circumstance. I want the reproduction, that dance inside Chagall´s canvas, its rustling, in order to conquer the horror of this fate and the blocks of mediocrity, the worst of all human illnesses. For you I want the festival, the apogee of its flight. I'm emotional and ridiculous.

In the street the deafening sound of a puncher drilling into the ground tortures my senses. Everything happens like that, between an ideal purpose and a reality plowing us under. We imagine nothing about the specific perfection that could nullify duality. Stop the mechanical clocks to "donner le change," he says, from the wall. Making change, putting on appearances. Always through an operation of the senses, never mechanically.

I thought about writing you a letter about indifference, another one about reason, some about celebrated women (Anaïs, Virginia, Clarisse, the Baroness von Blixen; Djuna Barnes, whose name we gave to the nasty cat). But I realized it was unnecessary. You'll seek your deceased friends out of destiny (out of displacement) and the story of that faraway Milena who descended into the hell of a Nazi concentration camp. To be free is to conquer the audacity of being a woman. Bringing her into an absolute present, here-now.

She's there on her postcard, sent from Germany by a stranger, unmoving in the night, stuck to the shelf with a tack. Her clear, serene eyes that have not revealed either torture or pain—only deep transparent

—la tortura ni el dolor, son un refugio. Acaban de mencionar a otra Milena en el programa de la radio, pero no se puede ser ni adquirir, a la distancia, otra Milena cualquiera.

"Si me permitiera elevar una simple súplica a Dios—dijo Katherin Mansfield—, dicha súplica sería *quiero ser real*." Yo, pediría lo contrario. No debes permitir ser más real que lo irreal. No debes dudar del elemento esencial que constituye nuestro destino, "verdadera libertad generadora de nuestro trabajo". No olvides tampoco, "que si aparece una abeja en tu sombrero, debes guardarla para hacer una colmena juntas", eso es lo irreal como producto de lo real. Todo lo bueno del ser y también del no ser, crece en el centro de esa advertencia que vigilamos en la noche, rodeamos por el día y necesitamos alcanzar en el después. Ellas se fundan, se trastocan, superponiendo esos hallazgos. En fin, busca las tijeras y recorta los versos. Busca la tela y recorta los brazos. Busca la cuquita y recorta un sentido de papel. Tú juegas a la vida, mientras la vida juega con su única carta, con crueldad y bondad, con esa maravilla de sentir a través de un papel tornasolado que ya no es reversible.

Parece que sólo ha pasado un segundo y, sin embargo, han pasado los años. ¡Te amo tanto! Siguen roturando la tierra. El corazón se quiere reconciliar con su sonido. Tengo la emoción del mayor desamparo en la palabra, roturando también la página. No somos sólo verbos, ¡sino sílabas de sustantivos vivos! Entramos en la página cuando estamos en el límite del aceite, en el límite de la lámpara, en el límite de todo. Y, al borde, pondré este epitafio que nunca fue reconocido, para que le sirva a todas las que fuimos, a todas las que seremos.

"Sé que de esta ortiga, el peligro, arrancaremos esta flor, la seguridad…" Es de alguien que no se sabe por fin existió, se llamaba Shakespeare (de niña, yo lo repetía en sílabas, Sha–kes–pea–re).

waters: a refuge. On the radio program they've just mentioned another Milena, but one can't be or acquire, across distance, just any other Milena.

"If I were allowed one simple cry to God," wrote Katherine Mansfield, "that cry would be I want to be REAL." I'd ask for the opposite. You shouldn't allow yourself to be more real than the unreal. Shouldn't doubt the essential element constituting our destiny, "real liberty generating our labor." And don't forget, "if a bee lands on your hat, you should protect it, to build a hive together": that's the unreal as a product of the real. All that is good about existence, and nonexistence too, grows in the heart of caution we observe throughout the night, enclose throughout the day, and need to realize afterwards. The women take their places then become disarranged, superimposing those discoveries. In short, look for scissors and trim out the lines. Look for the fabric and trim out arms. Look for the doll and trim a meaning from her paper. You play at life, while life plays with its only letter in cruelty and kindness, in that marvel of feeling through a glossy paper, irreversible.

It seems as though only a second has passed, and yet it has been years. I love you so much! They keep on punching at the ground. The heart tries to reconcile itself to the sound. I feel a great homelessness in the word, punching at the page too. We're not just verbs. We're syllables from living nouns! We enter the page when we're at the edge of the oil, the edge of the lamp, the edge of it all. And at the edge I'll put down this never-recognized epitaph, so it will serve all the women we were, all the ones we'll be.

"I tell you, out of this nettle, danger, we pluck this flower, safety…" It's from someone whose existence has never been confirmed, named Shakespeare (as a child, I repeated his name in four syllables, Shah–kess–peh–reh).

Una casa de Ánimas

La calle está perdida
bajo el humo del edificio más alto
y el edificio es casi un espejo cóncavo
donde puedo ver cómo crecí
desde el día en que nos separamos.

En la azotea de enfrente
una muchacha blanquísima
mira de reojo al hombre
que duerme desnudo en el espacio.
Apacigua la tormenta pasajera con los dedos,
pero no puede inaugurar esta calle
no tiene un pañuelo para despedirla.
Calle, dolor, hundimiento,
¡todo ha sido aquí representado!

¿Cuántas veces reflejada en la sábana
por encima del charco
he querido también, saltar?
¿Cuántas veces la desdicha ante el deseo incumplido
rechaza mi constancia?

La calle dobla frente a ti (juega)
se esconde en otra esquina.
Te esquiva fingiendo una curva, una impaciencia
—rara sinuosidad vencida por el ojo
postergando una definición tardía,
un olvido.

Busca una concha de nube nacarada
que no sea un simulacro.
Busca aquellos paisajes donde fuimos esclavos
de alguna belleza o bondad en ciertas tardes
contra la mansedumbre de creer
en las palabras
y sus dioses
boca abajo.

Mientras otra muchacha coloca su sábana impoluta
sobre un suelo manchado.

A House on Ánimas

The street is lost
under smoke from the tallest building
and the building is all but concave, a mirror
where I see how I've grown
since the day we diverged.

On the opposite rooftop
a superlatively white girl
looks askance at a man
sleeping in space, naked.
She lulls the passing storm with her fingers
but can't inaugurate this road
without a scarf for seeing it off.
Street, anguish, foundering—
everything has been represented here!

Reflected on the sheet laid over a pool of liquid
how many times
have I wanted, too, to jump?
How many times has discontent from some dubious desire
turned my faithfulness away?

Street turns in front of you (plays)
lurks on another corner.
Sidesteps you, fakes a curve, an impatience
—strange sinuosity overcome by the eye
putting off a belated definition,
a forgetting.

Go look for a shell of pearlized cloud
that would be no simulacrum.
Seek landscapes where we were slaves
to some grace or tenderness on certain afternoons,
defying the docility of believing
in words
and their gods
face down.

As another girl lays her untainted sheet
over a stained piece of ground.

Una ciudad puede ser una calle. Una arteria recortada por la que uno ha transitado desde la niñez. Cada vez que veo la calle Ánimas —la calle de las Ánimas— desde mi balcón, desde el tiempo transcurrido entre su poca extensión, su profuso trajín y mi mirada, se concentra el elemento simbólico de mi infancia. En sus cambios, en sus construcciones (más bien en su actual destrucción) están las huellas también de mi vida.

Es una calle como cualquiera, rota. Comienza con el Prado y sus leones de bronce oscurecidos por el tiempo mirando hacia el Palacio de los Matrimonios, un edificio de piedra ocre o palacete, donde se concentra lo más ceremonial y a la vez kitsch de la sociedad habanera. Al pasar frente a la escalera central por donde suben los novios —la cola de tul de la novia pisoteada por la turba de padrinos y amigos (y sobre todo de curiosos)—, uno siente la variedad olorosa de aquellos perfumes baratos destapados para esta ceremonia.

Podríamos decir que mi calle —la calle de las ánimas solas, de las almas que iban a morir al lado opuesto y final después de una pequeña, pero enorme trayectoria de dolor, ahora van directo al famoso hospital que la culmina desde su altura, quizás para salvarse. Pudiéramos decir, repito, que la calle Ánimas comienza su recorrido con un hecho nupcial y termina con la muerte o la resurrección. Que su tránsito es el tiempo que las almas piden para su redención. Que la boda y la muerte la celebran desde cada esquina donde los fotógrafos y los notarios convierten a los seres, moribundos o novios, por un instante irreal, en actores.

Sé que con esta calle, como pretexto inmerecido y biográfico se pueden decepcionar. Es estrecha aunque las hay peores. Algo intermedia y paralela siempre al mar. Aunque por su cercanía uno la puede también oler. (Ahora, los perfumes se mezclan además con la sal y se hacen salobres.)

Después de guardar los trajes alquilados para la ceremonia —la fanfarria y el oropel de los tules y zapatos con lentejuelas; los guantes sudados por el intenso calor; tintes que resplandecen enrojecidos al mediodía sobre peinados pasados de moda y toda clase de fantasía inimaginable, mandada muchas veces, o casi siempre, por los familiares de la novia que residen en "Mayami"—; en esa esquina, repito, se concentra un núcleo bien desfavorecido de la población. Sus edificios, en condiciones miserables, hablan desde las múltiples tendederas que cuelgan restos de todos los naufragios, cuando al mirar hacia el cielo de un azul casi de postal, en un día de verano brumoso en el que las nubes se hacen piedras blancas y fijas contra la mirada, alguien salta por sobre

A city can be a street. An artery identified by the road one has walked since childhood. Every time I see Ánimas Street—*the street of the spirits*—from my balcony, I peer through the time elapsed along its short span, through its prolific bustling and my line of sight; and the symbolic element of my childhood comes into focus. Traces of my life are present in its changes, in its constructions (better said: in its current state of destruction).

It's a street like any other, broken up. Ánimas begins with the Prado, with time-darkened bronze lions looking off toward the Palace of Matrimonies, a mansion or building of ochre stone, where the most ceremonial and simultaneously kitschy aspects of Havana society concentrate. When you pass the central stair where the couples ascend —the bride's tulle train crushed underfoot by a crowd of attendants and friends (and curious onlookers, more than anyone)—you smell the fragrant collection of cheap perfumes uncorked for this ceremony.

We could say that my street—the street for solitary spirits, souls who move toward death on the other and definitive end, after a brief but protracted trajectory of suffering—now they go straight to the famous hospital with which the street culminates, at an elevated point; perhaps they'll be saved. We could say, said differently, that Ánimas begins its journey with a nuptial event and ends in death or resurrection. That its passage is the passage of time souls request for their redemption. That marriage and death celebrate the road from every corner where, for one unreal instant, photographers and notaries transform beings, dying or betrothed, into actors.

I know that this street, as a biographical pretext, is unearned and disappointing. It's narrow, but others are worse. Middling, it merely runs parallel to the sea, though one can always smell water close by. (Now perfumes mix with salt, turn brackish.)

After packing away the suits rented for the ceremony—fanfare and glitter of tulle and spangled shoes; gloves soaked with sweat in intense heat; dyes glowing red at noon on outmoded hairstyles; and all imaginable fantasy details, sent over often, or almost always, by the bride's relatives who live in "Mayami"—; on that corner, to rephrase, a nucleus of the population truly lacking in privileges comes together. Their buildings, in miserable condition, speak through many illegal wires, rigged up as around all shipwrecks. On a misty summer day with clouds like white stone anchored against one's gaze, someone looks up at a sky nearly as blue as a postcard, then leaps out of this print with

nuestra impresión y grita, con un grito abierto y bienaventurado… "hay cielo empedrado", convirtiendo las piedras que empiezan a caer, o que en cualquier momento caerán, en pura imaginación. Entonces, parece que fuera a llover, y no cae más que el agua de la ropa mojada en los cordeles, como un rocío artificial que a la vez bendice a los novios y a sus invitados.

Después de la ceremonia todos quieren seguramente celebrar (más si se trata de la boda donde uno de los cónyuges es un extranjero). En la esquina próxima hay una Paladar de cuatro mesas de hierro y comida cubana: yuca con mojo, lechón y congrí: El Fénix, algo más arriba y con aire acondicionado. Aquí también venden pescados buenos y mariscos a hurtadillas (o sea, la langosta de manera clandestina). Con el pollo relleno de queso y jamón se puede almorzar, llevar para la casa y también comer, incluso compartir los huesos con el perro.

II

La calle de las Ánimas es una calle bruja. Las aceras se llenan de "cartuchos" que han reventado a las tres de la tarde para hacer el bien, o a las tres de la madrugada para hacer el mal. Un mercado clandestino de viejos y de mulatas sentados en los quicios de sus casas—o en pequeños bancos de madera de pino—te acosa al pasar con vegetales, huevos y plátanos. La gente camina y vende—calle arriba, calle abajo —todo lo que puede. Ya que por aquí, no pasan en la actualidad rutas de "guaguas". Antes pasaba la ruta 57 y paraba justo debajo de mi casa. Yo la seguía con un reloj infantil cuando era niña y con mi hermano jugábamos a los inspectores. Pero más recuerdo (a la ruta 57) de aquella época de mi adolescencia, cuando todavía iban vacías o quedaba siempre algún asiento posible. Después de la muerte de mi padre la cogíamos todas las noches. Llegábamos hasta el final y regresábamos en ella—dos, tres veces—, mi madre, mi hermano y yo, en un mismo asiento, apretujados hasta el cansancio, hasta que nos entrara con el aire de la noche el sueño necesario para olvidar la muerte. Pudiera decir también que la calle Ánimas se hizo para el paso triunfal de la ruta 57, y el estremecimiento del piso floreado de edificios tan antiguos, sobrevivientes al sonido perforador de su llegada desde Belascoaín hasta Prado, anunciando que éramos una ciudad con autobuses y todo. Hace muchos años que la 57 no pasa por aquí alumbrando las noches a través de las ventanas.

III

El mejor conocimiento de las cosas—ha dicho alguien seguramente antes que yo—pasa por la detección de sus formas, cómo se elaboran

the open and benedictory shout, "A cobblestone sky… "—transporting stones that are starting to fall, or will fall down at any moment, into the realm of pure imagination. Then rain seems likely; but the only falling water drips from wet clothes on lines, an artificial dew blessing the bride, the groom, and their guests.

After the ceremony everyone probably wants to celebrate (all the more if the bride or groom is a foreigner). On the next corner there's a small, privately owned restaurant with four iron tables and Cuban food: yucca with lemon and garlic sauce, suckling pig, beans and rice. The Phoenix, a bit farther along, comes with air conditioning. Here they sell good fish and "sneaky seafood" (lobster acquired in clandestine ways). You can lunch on chicken stuffed with ham and cheese, take some home with you to eat, share the bones with your dog.

II

The Street of The Souls is bewitching. Her sidewalks fill with "runners" who roll out at three in the afternoon to do good, or three in the morning to do evil. A clandestine market comprised of old men and mulattas, seated on the stoops of their homes—or small pine benches—harasses you, as you pass by, with vegetables, eggs, and plaintains. Up one street and down another, people walk and sell anything they can. Because "guaguas," the buses, no longer use this street for their routes. The 57 used to go through here, stopping just below my home. As a little girl I timed it with a child's watch, playing bus inspector with my brother. But I remember more about the 57 from my adolescence, when buses still went past empty, or some seat was always open. After my father's death we took the 57 every night. We'd ride out to the end of the line, then come back around—two, three circuits—my mother, my brother and I, sharing a seat, squeezed together until exhaustion set in, until we took in enough sleepiness with the night air to forget about death. You could say that Ánimas Street was made for the triumphal return along the 57's route, with the thrill of the flowered floors in its antiquated buildings. They survived the drilling noise made by the 57's arrivals from Belascoaín down to Prado, announcing that we were a city with buses and everything. Many years have passed since the 57 stopped going by, illuminating night through the windows.

III

The best way of knowing things—someone surely said this before me—is in one's own movement through detection of their forms, how forms

49

y reproducen en la memoria personal (y también colectiva) a través del tiempo. Mi calle ha tenido ese privilegio, las demás eran, simplemente, puras calles. Los ciclos de mi vida, sus calendarios; cada paso de acercamiento o de alejamiento que la calle va borrando y que a la vez va construyendo, determina su otredad. Su manera de influir en nuestros días y en nuestras noches. El recorrido que logra ser siempre el mismo. Es mentira que queramos coger por calles diferentes porque nos asustan. Pueden desviarnos del mapa diario, de lo que en nuestra calle aconteció o faltó, de lo que perseguimos desde la noche a la mañana, y de lo que logramos o perdimos desde la primera vuelta hasta el fin: la huella de nuestros pasos marcando un territorio como hacen los gatos, descolorido y mental.

IV

La identidad se recrea en un proceso latente y semántico: nombro mi calle, mi calle me contiene. A veces entro en ella y no la recuerdo, no la reconozco, se me pierde—o la escondo—para volver a nombrarla. Ahí se paraliza la concepción profunda de sostener una ciudad ante todas las otras externas concepciones, el costo de un edificio, sus transformaciones. Las sinuosidades del neobarroco, su claroscuro, no tiene más existencia que en una iluminación íntima. Recorro este borde, me recuesto en esta puerta—alguien mira por la persiana hecha con maderas vulgares y de adquisición reciente—, el vértigo de la piedra cuando cae y se desploma contra el asfalto existe muy adentro, porque afuera nada existe.

V

La calle Ánimas no tiene un solo árbol que garantice su sombra o frescor. La luz—si bien no cae directamente—tampoco propicia suficiente sombra. Las aceras están rotas y poco barridas. Los basureros se desbordan y lo que antes fuera el edificio más antiguo de Ánimas y San Nicolás, de una vuelta por la esquina se fue cayendo poco a poco, al no mirarlo, al no poder detenerlo con mis brazos, y ahora se convirtió en un mercado popular. Esta calle cada vez me produce más desconcierto. No tiene recursos para el desarrollo de las identidades locales. Es una calle muy pobre. ¿Cómo pretenderé salvarla? ¿Qué le doy? Hay una plaquita en la casa contigua a la mía donde estuvo la primera emisora de radio (CMQ) con los nombres de los que allí trabajaron, directores, locutores, artistas… También estuvo el Instituto del Libro cuando Alejo Carpentier era su director. Recuerdo que Puci—su secretaria—se cosía

are elaborated and reproduced in personal memory (and collective memory) over time. My street has been privileged in this manner, while the other ones were just streets. Cycles of my life, its calendars; each step moving towards or away from something—which the street goes about erasing and simultaneously constructing—determines its otherness. Its way of influencing our days and nights. Course that manages to be the same every time. Any statement that we want to test out different roads is a lie, because they scare us. They can detour us from our daily map, from what did or didn't happen on our street, from what we pursue from nightfall until dawn, and from what we achieve or lose between the first lap and the finish: trace of our steps marking out a territory, like cats—a territory faded, and of the mind.

IV

Identity recreates itself in a latent and semantic process: I name my street, my street contains me. Sometimes I go out on the street and don't remember or recognize it, the street is lost—or I conceal it—so I can return to the act of naming it. There, paralysis sets in when the deep concept about sustaining a city meets other external conceptions, the cost of a building, its transformations. Sinuosities of the neobaroque, its chiaroscuro—it has no existence outside an interior enlightenment. I travel along this borderline, I sit down in this doorway—someone peers through blinds made from rough, recently acquired wood—the rock's vertigo while falling, exploding against the asphalt, exists deep inside. Because outside, nothing exists.

V

Ánimas Street doesn't have a single tree to lend it cool or shade. Since its light doesn't fall directly, it doesn't provide adequate shadow. The sidewalks are broken and rarely swept. Garbage dumps overflow; the building at Ánimas and San Nicolás, once the oldest, and just around the corner, collapsed piece by piece. I couldn't protect it, couldn't hold it in place with my arms. The site was converted into a street market. This road makes me feel more and more uncertain. It has no resources for the development of local identities. It's a deeply impoverished road. How will I attempt to save it? What do I offer to this road? There's a little plaque on the house next to mine where the first radio broadcast station (CMQ) once was, presenting names of the people who worked there: directors, announcers, artists... The Book Institute was also there, when Alejo Carpentier directed it. I remember Puci—his secretary—who

con mi madre y me traía cajas de libros recién publicados. Antologías del cuento polaco, del cuento norteamericano…, del cuento ruso. Yo hacía reposo por la desviación de la columna (también por la desviación que encontré en esta vida, en esta calle). Resultaba diferente a lo que siempre había pensado. No moría en Belascoaín, sino que hacía una curva, una ligera sinuosidad que continuaba donde podía ser ya, otra calle: la otra. Pero esa no le pertenecía a mi mirada. A pesar de su escoliosis (mi calle), la que me pertenecía desde siempre, terminaba conmigo desde el balcón.

VI

Hoy le pregunto a Fillo que vive aquí hace 31 años; a Isabel que vive hace 50 y pico (yo vivo hace 41). Casi todos recordamos el bar Lulú de la acera de enfrente. Lo recordábamos por sus escándalos—yo era bien niña entonces pero sentía el miedo que tenía mi madre por ese bar de enfrente, lujurioso—. El bar era casi sólo el espacio de un balcón donde se apretujaban las putas y los borrachos. Cada noche sentíamos el escándalo, ahora ese bar no existe. El escándalo está en la calle y las "broncas" de la calle Ánimas y San Nicolás son a machete o, con sacapuntas, casi siempre broncas viejas entre familias. "Mucho ruido y pocas nueces"—como dicen aquí—. Todo el mundo se sabe la vida del otro al dedillo. Yo doblo siempre por San Nicolás y no llego a Manrique, sino que cojo por Virtudes—las virtudes me interesan más y parecen pacíficas—.

VII

No obstante tanta precariedad, tenemos algunos edificios, algunas máscaras y una estatua principal. La estatua de la casa de enfrente, la que vigila todos mis actos: la verdadera espía, es ella. Vigila "mi desamor, mi desconfianza". Es una estatua de mármol (una buena reproducción) y, aunque está en un primer piso en el interior de una casa, se ve desde la calle. Cuando uno está muy solo se detiene a mirar la estatua. Es raro encontrar estatuas dentro de los edificios de vivienda y sobre todo de este tamaño. Mirándola bien comprendo que siempre la he visto más como un personaje que como una estatua pero, para el que viene y la ve, debe ser algo bien extraño, en fin, una estatua colosal dentro de una casa de vecindad. La casa donde está colocada tiene hundimiento, pero la estatua la salva, la sobredimensiona. Algo también sirve en la estatua para glorificar la calle y darle cierta aristocracia. La estatua sobre pisos floreados, de principios de siglo. Baila.

used to sew with my mother, and she brought me boxes of recently published books. Anthologies of Polish stories, Northamerican stories…, Russian stories. I had to rest at home due to a curvature of the spine (and curvature I found in this life, in this street). It turned out differently than I'd always thought. I wasn't dying on Belascoaín; instead I was forming a curve, a faint sinuosity that continued where there might be another street already: the other girl. But she didn't belong to my line of sight. In spite of its scoliosis (my street), the one that always belonged to me, she was ending her connection with me, as seen from that balcony.

VI

Today I have questions for Fillo, who has lived here for 31 years, and Isabel, who has been here for more than fifty (me, 41). Almost everyone remembers Bar Lulu across the street. We remembered Lulu for its scandals—I was very young then, but I sensed my mother's fear of that bar facing us, licentious. The bar took up little more than the space of a balcony where prostitutes and drunks pressed together. Every night we felt its indecency. Lulu no longer exists. Indecency has moved out to the street, and the spats of Ánimas and San Nicolás involve machetes, or the pencils of sharp arguments between families, usually old disagreements. "Great big noise, very few nuts"—as they say here. Everyone knows their neighbors' lives intimately. I always turn off at San Nicolás and don't go all the way to Manrique, but take Virtudes instead—Virtudes, The Virtues, interest me more; they seem peaceful.

VII

So precarious. Nevertheless, we have some buildings, some masks, and a reigning statue. The statue in the house out front, the one who watches all my actions: the real spy, that's her. She patrols "my lack of affection, my distrust." She's a marble statue (fine reproduction) and, although she's located on the second floor of the interior of a house, she's visible from the street. When one is very much alone, one pauses to look at the statue. It's strange to find statues inside buildings that are working households, especially statues of this size. Looking at her carefully, I understand that I've always seen her more as a character than a statue, but for the person who sees her in passing, she must be truly odd: a colossal statue within a residential home. The house where she is located has undergone some sinking, but the statue saves the house, she gives it buoyancy. Something about the statue also serves to glorify the street, lending it a certain aristocracy. Statue, poised above flowers set into floors, from the beginning of a century. She dances.

VIII

Mi escritura es el recorrido de mis ojos por lo que nunca he dejado de ver aunque salga y vuelva, aunque me esconda. La verdadera página de estos acontecimientos que no han sucedido, que simplemente fueron expresión de un delirio. La calle-página es también como un zíper abierto en medio de la espalda, debajo del cual sobresale un cuerpo aprisionado, una razón que descubrir. Cuando llego a la esquina me espanto de que mi vida, durante tantos años, haya transcurrido aquí, y no saber realmente si la habré conocido, si me ha visto pasar por ella.

VIII

My writing is the route my eyes trace down the thing I've never stopped seeing, even if I go away and return, even if I retreat. The actual page for events that haven't happened, being no more than the expression of my delirium. The street-page is also like a zipper running open down the length of one's back, out of which an imprisoned body surges, a motive for discovery. When I get to the corner I feel alarmed. My life has played out here for so many years, but I'm not sure I even know my corner: I don't know whether it ever saw me moving down this road.

Diotima

He viajado hacia atrás con el pensamiento… hasta regiones remotas
en las que busqué a tientas alguna salida, aunque sólo para descubrir
que la prisión del tiempo es esférica y carece de ellas…
V. Nabokov

Diotima murió el 18 de febrero del 2002, durante esos días en que los brujos reunidos en Ginebra pronosticaban, cosas terribles a la humanidad. Estaba como cada anochecer, acurrucada entre mi hombro y el antebrazo. Sonó el teléfono, me levanté. No sabré nunca qué pasó afuera. Un ruido sordo, abajo. Los muchachos gritaban desde el segundo piso. Ella, aparentemente, se enredó con una cabilla suelta en el alero y cayó al centro de la calle. La enterraron en una funda blanca. He tratado de reconstruir todos estos años, cada detalle de lo que aconteció entre nosotras.

Con Diotima comienza y termina un ciclo de mi vida, aún hoy, cuando lo recuerdo y lo escribo, me tiembla el pulso. No tuve fuerzas para verla morir ni para concebir su muerte. Siempre pensé que viviría tanto o más que yo. El vacío que deja es una mancha blanca superpuesta detrás de mí, cuando abro o cierro la puerta, subo o bajo un peldaño, amanece, anochece. Sólo ella, mi gata y única amiga, sabía dormir a mi lado.

Veo sus patas delanteras estirarse confirmándome que aún sigue allí, después de su baño, al despertar. He puesto una foto, un búcaro con flores frente a un cuadro donde estamos. Volví una semana después al sitio donde la enterraron. El viento y la lluvia habían revolcado la tierra dejándola semi enterrada. Busqué una pala (es difícil hallar una pala en esta ciudad para enterrar algo). Busqué dos hombres que me ayudaron a enterrarla, profundamente, y después de unos minutos, regresé más tranquila. A veces, paso, miro. Quisiera plantar un árbol, poner un columpio para los niños, hacer un parque allí. Diotima se quedó muy sola la noche del 18 de febrero, y yo también.

Cuando uno admite que un animal semisiamés, de ojos pequeños y bizcos (azul pálido), es más importante que cualquier ser; cuando uno admite que ha muerto en ese animal un alma, se establece un problema para el resto de las especies y, sobre todo, para los mortales humanos. Diotima no sonreía ni podía sonreír, pero sus ojos, de una fijeza y calma inigualables, sabían sostener la mirada.

Puso a sus hijos junto a mi almohada, con lo que me vi obligada durante sus cuatro partos a poner una cesta junto a mi cabecera, donde ella quería que se quedaran y, luego, a criarlos. Confiaba en mí.

Diotima

*I have journeyed back in thought ... to remote regions where I
groped for some secret outlet only to discover that the prison
of time is spherical and without exits ...*[*]
V. Nabokov

Diotima died on 18 February 2002, during the days when seers gathered
in Geneva were predicting terrible things for humanity. As on every
evening, she was curled up between my shoulder and forearm. The
phone rang, I got up. I'll never know what happened outside. A muffled
sound below. The guys shouted out from the third floor. Apparently she
got tangled up with a loose bar on the roof and fell down to the middle of
the street. They buried her in a white pillowcase. Over the years I've tried
to reconstruct every detail of what took place between us.

A cycle of my life begins and ends with Diotima; even today,
as I remember and write about it, my pulse speeds up. I didn't have the
strength to watch her die or even imagine her death. I always thought
she would live as long as me, or longer. The emptiness she leaves be-
hind is a white spot stamped behind me when I open or close the door,
step up or down the stairs, get up, go to sleep. Only Diotima, my cat and
sole female friend, slept by my side.

I see her front paws stretch, confirming that she's still here,
after a morning bath. I put a photo, a vase of flowers under a picture of
us. A week afterwards I returned to the site where they buried her. Wind
and rain had displaced the dirt, leaving her only partly interred. I looked
for a spade (it's hard to find a spade in this city to use for burial). I found
two men who helped me to bury her, deep, and after a few minutes I
went home feeling more calm. Sometimes I walk by and look. I'd like to
plant a tree, put up a swing for children, build a park there. Diotima was
left very much alone that night, February 18, and so was I.

When one accepts that a part-Siamese animal, with small
(pale blue) squinty eyes, is more important than any other being; when
one accepts that a soul has died in this animal; it generates a problem
for other species and above all for mortal humans. Diotima didn't
smile, nor could she smile, but her eyes, with unparalleled firmness
and calm, could sustain a gaze. She placed her offspring next to my
pillow, obligating me during her four deliveries to put a basket by my
headboard, where she wanted them to stay, and to care for them. She
trusted me.

[*]From the first chapter of *Speak, Memory*.

En este año 2002 y con su muerte, a los doce años de nacida y de su llegada a mi casa, en el mes de febrero también, se cierra todo lo que el tiempo me permitió construir (una casa, mi hija, una gata).

Prisionera de sus recorridos, nunca supe dónde hacía la caca, de tan pulcra y reservada como era. Supongo que en la buganvilla morada, pero no estoy segura.

Muchas veces saltó del tejado al sentirme llorar, toser o sangrar. Eduardo Subirats, el filósofo, presenció durante una visita que me hizo, cómo mientras me desangraba, Diotima se desesperaba a mi lado y se ponía casi a punto de hablar. Y hablaba, en sus diez y seis sonidos anteriores al habla y me decía con sus ojos, con su lengua áspera, "te amo, yo te amo", más, mucho más, que cualquier persona.

No supe, no pude, o no quise tener amigas. Siempre ha sido imposible para mí, entregarme a la confianza de otras mujeres. Las amistades femeninas fueron cada vez más limitadas y sólo pasaron a convertirse en conversaciones telefónicas y esporádicas. Achaco esto a mi desconfianza, a mi egoísmo, y a la sustitución que hice por las mujeres muertas de los anaqueles. En cambio, Diotima llenó absolutamente ese vacío. En los tiempos difíciles, no sólo crió a sus hijos, sino que me ayudó a criar a los míos con las cachetadas de sus patas delanteras durante las peleas domésticas en las que siempre intervino.

Nunca se rindió. Aprendió a sentarse, a esperar, a no tener desasosiego.

Antes de salir para algún viaje, se metía de tal manera en la maleta que llevaba clavadas las uñas en la piel, como marcas de una fidelidad a prueba de cualquier distancia. También en la ropa dejaba una huella: sus benditos pelos blancos.

¿A quién puede interesarle que al cerrar el círculo una vida, el acontecimiento más fuerte haya sido la muerte de una gata?

Fuimos compañeras de este viaje, juego, ocasión, fingimiento de existir. Ningún animal ni persona podría sustituirla ahora. Pasamos dolores, rabias, hambre, sueños, amores, desamores y, sobre todo, el proceso de envejecer juntas. Crecieron su vientre y el mío, se ablandaron sus uñas tanto como las mías. Nacimos para habitar el tercer piso de una casa de Ánimas y ella, antes de enfermar para morir, decidió caer, sobrevolar, fingir que quieta, en calma, así como vivió, quedaría intacta en mi mente.

He tenido otros gatos, otros animales a lo largo de mi vida. Fieles y hermosos, también malos y feos, pero ninguno supo colocarse en el lugar exacto de mi respiración, acompasarse conmigo a ese círculo que se llama existencia.

In this year, 2002, with her death twelve years after her birth and arrival at my home, which also occurred in the month of February, everything closes: everything time allowed me to create (a house, my daughter, a cat).

Prisoner of her paths: I never did find out where she pooped, she was so tidy and reserved. I suppose it was in the purple bougainvillea. But I'm not sure.

She often jumped down from the roof when she sensed I was crying, sneezing or bleeding. During a visit philosopher Eduardo Subirats noticed how Diotima behaved at my side as I bled, so upset that she was on the point of speaking. And she spoke, in her sixteen sounds preceding speech, and said with her eyes, her rough tongue, "I love you, I love you"—more, much more, than any person.

I never learned how, or couldn't learn, or didn't want to have female friends. It has always been impossible for me to trust other women. Feminine friendships became ever more limited and turned into sporadic phone calls. I attribute this to my lack of trust, my egoism, and substitution with dead women off my bookshelves. By contrast Diotima filled that void completely. During the hard times she didn't just raise her offspring but helped me to raise mine, with swipes of her front paws in domestic squabbles, in which she always intervened.

She never wore out. She learned how to sit down, how to wait, how not to be anxious.

Before my trips, she got into the suitcase and dug her nails into the leather, like marks of loyalty strong enough to stand up to any distance. She also left her trace on clothing: strands of her blessed white fur.

Who would be interested by the fact that upon the closing of one life's circle, the most powerful event has been the death of a cat?

We were companions on this trip, game, occasion, simulated existence. No animal or person could replace her now. We lived through sorrows, rages, hunger, dreams, loves, indifference, and above all, the process of growing old together. Her womb grew and so did mine, her nails softened as much as mine. We were born to inhabit the fourth floor of a home on Ánimas, and before she could die of illness she decided to fall, fly over, pretend she is appeased, at peace; in my mind she remained as she lived.

I've had other cats, other animals throughout the course of my life. Loyal and lovely, as well as naughty and unattractive, but none of the others learned how to align with the exact location of my breath, to synchronize with me in that circle named existence.

La voz del Niágara

En aquel pueblito de postal había una voz. Hasta entrada ya al sitio, en el preámbulo, diría yo, el sonido era sólo una diferencia o aquella bruma que se veía tan lejana, al centro.

El agua cae y me hace sentir su latigazo. El cielo está bajito y limpio, puramente azul. No parecía nada hacia los alrededores de aquello, inmenso parque o jardín, pero que en verdad, no era ni una ni otra cosa, un sitio extraño. Y de pronto, el abismo de agua congelada arrasa con la visión.

Allí estaban grabados los versos de Heredia, el poeta cubano que inmortalizó las cataratas. Las palabras de Heredia son como hielos cortantes. Agua espumosa hecha de humo, congelada después. Hay muy pocos turistas y una pareja que se atreve a bajar hacia el acantilado donde los diminutos botes ánforas saltan contra la corriente y atraviesan una zona oscura, donde el golpe de agua aterra.

Después de esta experiencia, tuve la sensación de nacer limpia. La catarata devela un misterio que no podré jamás descifrar. Ningún paisaje podrá encerrarla para disminuir sus actos centrífugos. La catarata se desborda hacia algo que no es sólo recuerdo: es permanencia de un estado dentro de nosotros, anticipación. Diluvio, ceremonia. Aún, muchas noches me desvelo sintiendo el sonido del vapor que cae al vacío desfigurando la serenidad del cielo. Dicen que en épocas más frías que en las que yo estuve allí, la catarata se congela completamente y se convierte en un árbol con ramas de cristal que bajan al abismo, un gran árbol que se corta al rente sin saber cómo ni dónde.

Las palabras del poeta, por grandes que sean, por inmortales que parezcan, no pueden sobrepasar mi visión ni aquel momento del estar allí. ¿La naturaleza es más poderosa que el lenguaje, entonces? No estoy segura, creo que el recuerdo de haber estado en ese sitio logra una relación interminable de sucesos que ya son lenguaje también y lo hacen inolvidable. La temperatura, el ruido que no se sabe de dónde proviene aunque se sepa, la textura del ambiente, el café que tomé, la manta que usé como abrigo, el tono a través de los espejuelos, todo se convierte en algo que no se puede definir, más que como un desafío a la comprensión, y una voz.

The Voice of the Niagara

There was a voice in that postcard village. Leading into the site, as a pre-amble, I'd say, the sound was just a difference, or the fog that seemed so distant, at the center.

The water falls and whips me with its lash. The sky is pale and clean, purely blue. Nothing stood out around that area, an immense park or garden, but really it was neither one thing nor another, a strange place. And suddenly the abyss of frozen water sweeps the view away.

Verses engraved there were written by Heredia, the Cuban poet who immortalized the waterfalls. His words cut like shards of ice. Foaming water made from smoke then frozen. A very few tourists are there, as well as a couple who dares to walk down toward the cliff: below, tiny boats, amphoras, toss against the current and cross through a dark area where the water lands terrifying blows.

After this experience I had the sensation of a clean rebirth. The waterfall reveals a mystery I never manage to decipher. No landscape could enclose it to diminish its centrifugal action. The waterfall over-flows toward something that isn't just memory: it is the permanence of a state within us, anticipation. Deluge, ceremony. Still, on many nights I can't sleep, hearing the sound of the vapor falling into the abyss, distort-ing the serenity of the sky. They say that in seasons colder than when I was there, the waterfall freezes completely, a tree with glass branches reaching down toward the abyss, a great tree crisscrossing itself with piled branches, without knowing how or where.

The words of the poet, great as they may be, immortal as they may seem, can't catch up to my vision or that moment of being there. Is nature more powerful than language, then? I'm not sure; I think the memory of having been in that place becomes charged with a nev-er-ending relation of events that now are language too, and they make it unforgettable. The temperature, the noise which comes from some location you can't find even when you know how, the textures of the environment, the coffee I drank, the blanket I used as a coat, the tone of mirages, it all turns into something you can't define except as a chal-lenge to comprehension, and a voice.

Alfiles

Mi padre murió sin alcanzar el título de "Campeón nacional de ajedrez". La fama no quiso acompañarlo hasta el final y murió dieciocho días después de haber cumplido los cincuenta años. Hoy, puedo comprender —muy cerca del arribo a esa edad la semana próxima— lo joven que él era. (Yo estaba acabada de cumplir catorce y mi hija cumplirá, ahora, los trece.) Mi padre se hallaba en el cenit de su carrera de ajedrecista, cuando un coágulo le hizo la trastada.

A una semana de mis cincuenta julios, lo recuerdo. Era un hombre atlético y vital, un jugador y amante empedernido. De él aprendí el gusto por las piedras, los colores, el mar, la altanería (pero en alguna trama, seguro, perdimos resistencia y hacemos tablas ahora, en la partida). No fue en el vicio ni en el amor (esa trampa de los sentidos quizás, mortal) aún no sé de qué carácter fue el error.

Después del vacío de su muerte y de la culpa que me persiguió por haberle dicho "egoísta" aquella mañana del primero de agosto en que lo vi, por última vez, a la distancia de los extremos de un pasillo alargado. Después de soportar muchas facetas jerarquizadas de esa culpa (que no es más que otra justificación o muletilla fácil para soportar ser "la víctima" de esa mandrágora que consume también, al padre), comprendo que sólo ha pasado un instante, un intervalo corto, entre su fin a los cincuenta años acabados de cumplir y mi proximidad a esa fecha que ya no es posible doblar como esta esquina del parque. Después, vino el olvido de mi padre.

Si el aferramiento (con todos los recovecos dolorosos, torturantes, de que somos capaces); si las sustituciones hechas poco a poco, no son más que aberraciones donde encontrar un eje o sostén para acampar (y en cuántos hombres o textos quise yo acampar, ver a mi padre, su perfil moreno, la caída muñeco-biscuit de sus pestañas), entonces, vino después el olvido. Lo arrinconamos para ser famosos por un rato, para distraernos contra las pérdidas.

No sé quién tiene hoy sus libros de ajedrez que por años permanecieron encerrados en un clóset, sus pinturas de santos, algunas cartas (sólo conservo una foto en un bote de remos que se llamaba *El Vencedor* donde él descubre un torso triunfal contra las olas). He hablado de su mejilla prieta, de un lunar abultado, de su colonia gris impregnada en las camisas McGregor; he hablado también de sus amantes, de las que ahora llevan el nombre las protagonistas de mis bocetos de novelas.

Pero todo esto que marca una defensa (una insuficiencia en la página)

Bishops

My father died without winning the title of National Chess Champion. That fame didn't accompany him in the end, and he died eighteen days after his fiftieth birthday. Today I can understand—closing in on my own arrival at that age next week—how young he was. (I had just turned fourteen then, and now my daughter is turning thirteen.) My father was at the peak of his career as a chess player when a blood clot did him wrong.

A week away from my fiftieth July, I'm remembering. He was an athletic man, full of life, a player and inveterate lover. From him I learned to take pleasure in stones, colors, the sea—and arrogance (but thanks to some twist we can't hold out, so we end our matches in draws). It wasn't about vice or love (that trap of the senses, perhaps, a mortal one); I still don't know what kind of error it was.

After the emptiness of his death and the guilt that plagued me for having called him "selfish" that morning on the first of August, when I saw him for the last time, across the distance separating two extremes of a lengthy hallway; after surviving many hierarchical layers of guilt (just another justification or easy filler for enduring one's status as "the victim" of a mandrake, which also consumes the father), I understand that only an instant has passed: a short interval between his end, having just turned fifty, and my approach to that age, from which it's no longer possible to turn away as if I were rounding this corner of the park. Afterwards came my forgetting of my father.

If the obstinacy (with all the torturous twists and turns of which we're capable); if the substitutions, made little by little; if these are all just digressions along which to find an axis, or supports under which I could camp (and in how many men or texts did I try to set up camp, try to see my father, his dark profile, the lovely biscuit-porcelain fall of his eyelashes)—then the forgetting followed. We set him aside in order to be renowned for a short time, to distract ourselves from the losses.

Today I don't know who has his chess books, which were stored inside a closet for years; or his paintings of saints, some letters (all I've saved is a photograph of him on a rowboat called *The Victor*, where he reveals a torso victorious against the waves). I've spoken about his dark-skinned cheek, about a large mole, about his graying hair and its pomade, which worked its way into the McGregor shirts; I've also spoken of his lovers, of the women whose names now appear as the protagonists in my sketches for novels. But all this, which delineates a defense (an insufficiency on the page) demonstrates that my father

demuestra que mi padre me enseñó lo que es vivir en el abandono de un padre. Mi padre, sin querer (sin proponérselo), y sin la menor culpa, por supuesto (voz de trueno que hacía retumbar los cristales del aparador), me enseñó con aquel grito de despedida ese límite (un abismo) que se llena con palabras abstractas, luego. Esa posición privilegiada que está entre el tener o no tener un padre. Y en ese abismo (un cuenco), como también podría llamarlo, he colocado a todos mis amantes, textos, desprendimientos —boronillas, ripios, pacotilla, cachivaches—, que juntos no logran alcanzar lo que perdí: el amor de mi padre.

La soledad que quedó después (porque la soledad antes de ser una palabra abstracta es un doblez en la página), susto o promesa de que no volverá la palabra "egoísta" que se desprende sin querer de la boca de la niña y se convierte en eco, de manera que uno no quiere saber más de su contenido ni articular su vulgar sonoridad, y quisiera quitarla del resto de las palabras mortales, porque nos deja un hueco en el estómago, una tripa pegada contra otra (un tajo), esa inmoralidad de hambre que se siente más tarde, cuando la comprendemos en toda su resonancia maligna y es sólo una página que aún no está hecha o marcada ni por su envés ni por ninguna parte, esperándonos para disculparnos un poco.

No he podido situar la fama de mi padre en un lugar de mi propia trayectoria. No he podido colocar en los terrenos, por los que él me aventuró, la piedra marfil con hocico de oso que encontramos en un cementerio de agua en Santa Fe aquella tarde, porque nunca más he vuelto allí o porque él nunca ha regresado. Porque no convencida de su muerte prematura, lo incluí en mi propio escenario robándome el suyo, más bien, ocultándolo. Porque no he tenido la fama (que es el coraje suficiente) para reivindicar su propia imagen sin apropiármelo, más que como repertorio cotidiano de quejas y de incapacidades.

Sólo una vez, pasando transversal a la esquina de El Encanto (la famosa tienda de Galiano y San Rafael convertida en parque después de un incendio que la consumió en segundos), cruzando en diagonal losetas perforadas por tantas pisadas, la estafa de estanque, los árboles arrancados por cualquier viento sur aciclonado, vi su doble sentado en un banco (el otro pedazo de padre que me quedó), pero, cuando retrocedí para buscarlo, ya no era él. Sólo un día, en un sueño, me llamó por teléfono y oí su voz, diciéndome la misma palabra con la que nos despedimos: "egoísta". Lo cierto es que nunca hice nada por reivindicar a mi padre y pretendí reconstruirlo, tragándomelo.

¡Pobre de mí! Por eso, él se ríe ahora con sus amantes muertas ("Ricitos de oro", las llamaba), con su colonia gris, con sus camisas de

taught me what it means to live after abandoning one's father. My father, accidentally (without setting out to do so), and of course without the slightest bit of guilt (thunderous voice rattling crystal pieces in the sideboard), taught me with his shouted goodbye about a space of limitation (an abyss) that eventually fills with abstract words. That privileged position: the one that lies between having and not having a father. And into that abyss (a hollow), as you could also call it, I've placed all my lovers, texts, detachables—leftovers, scraps, gimcracks, garbage-picked and recycled objects—which even all together can't add up to what I lost: my father's love.

The solitude that remained afterwards (because solitude, before becoming an abstract word, is a fold on the page), fright or promise that there will be no return of the word "selfish," which accidentally emerges from the girl's mouth and turns into an echo, so one doesn't want to know any more about its content or articulate its vulgar resonance —in fact would like to take it out and away from the rest of the mortal words—because it leaves us with a hole in the stomach, one intestine squashed against the next (a slit), an immorality in the hunger one feels later, when we understand it in all its malignant resonance: just a page that still hasn't been created or marked, not on its flip side or anywhere else, waiting to offer us a little mercy.

I haven't been able to place my father's reputation into my own trajectory. Nowhere on the terrains through which he propelled me have I been able to find that chunk of marble with a bear snout, which we found in a watery grave one afternoon in Santa Fe. Because I've never gone back there, or because he never returned. Because, unconvinced about his early death, I included him in my own scenario, robbing it from him for myself, or better said, hiding him. Because I haven't had the reputation (which is the sufficient temerity) to vindicate his image without appropriating it for myself, beyond an everyday repertory of complaints and inabilities.

Only once, cutting across the corner by El Encanto (the famous store at Galiano and San Rafael streets, turned into a park after a fire consumed the building in a few seconds), walking a diagonal over tiles perforated by so many footsteps, the fraud of a pond, trees torn out by whatever hurricane-level winds from the south—only once did I see his double seated on a bench (the other piece I still held of my father) but, when I went back to look for him, that man wasn't him anymore. One day in a dream, he called me on the phone and I heard his voice, saying the same word to me with which we said our goodbye: "selfish." The indisputable part is that I never did anything to revive my father, and I tried to reconstruct him, swallowing him up.

seda, cuando pongo una copa con un marpacífico sobre el armario (por allí entrará cuando pase la fumigación, pienso) y vigilo si la lagartija que se esconde también y me engaña, habrá sobrevivido después de estos inventos de humareda y salvación para seres que pretenden tener dobles, fantasmas.

Quizás, mi padre volverá por el reflejo del agua en la cubeta plástica, puesta para las goteras del techo, o se esconderá en la borra del café mezclado o entrará por otros "andamios del querer" (mala metáfora) salvando esa distancia que nos ha tomado treinta y siete años, miles de sílabas de incomprensión, broncas y sustituciones imposibles para algún campeonato de simultáneas jamás realizado (con estilo o sin él) y donde no habrá tampoco vencedores.

Nariz y mejilla prietas. Papelitos sobrantes de los regalos vacíos de mis cumpleaños guardados en cajitas chinas con formas nostálgicas de pirámide con palacios pintados a mano que nunca visité. Lazos de tafetán rajándose ante mis ojos dentro de una gaveta de la cómoda antigua. Etiquetas pegajosas en sus camisas (aún con la marca invisible de los besos con "pintalabios" que otras le daban). No son más que malas metáforas de un padre, ridículos envoltorios para sobrevivirlo. Pero me quedó una cosa importante, la mejor cosa que me enseñó a ser impresionista desde entonces: esta esquina llamada también La Esquina del Pecado desde donde lo contemplo todavía en un rostro equivocado.

La tienda ha desaparecido con sus vidrieras, sus frágiles muñecas italianas y departamentos para encargos donde se vendían ilusiones, artículos, curiosidades y hasta aquellas medias Casino que compré para que se las pusiera en el baile de mis quince años (las que nunca se pudo poner). Pero, aunque me vaya o me distraiga, dé la vuelta en la chiva que hace, con su carretón ordinario y otro animal más joven, el mismo recorrido por el escenario del parque, sigo sentada para sostener todo aquello que fue mi infancia. Los restos de un edificio art decó (paredes manoseadas) por el lujo de pensar que al quedarme y mirarlo, su fondo cuarteado caerá también sobre la página si regreso y ya no está.

Entonces, mi padre dijo: "… vengan siempre aquí cuando yo no esté…" y esa fue la última vez que visitamos Santa Fe. Para lograr retener algo, había que dar la contraorden.

¡Era tan feliz cuando tocaba aquel guayo plateado que un anciano me dejó (el de la foto) que sonaba como un caracol vacío y brillante! ¿Puedo rescatar aquel sonido al rallar con una piedra del derrumbe, el texto? ¿Por qué se fueron esas cosas que ahora vuelven con intermiten-

Poor me! So now he laughs with his dead lovers ("Goldilocks," he called them), with what I called his "gray-hair pomade," with his silk shirts, when I put a cup with a red hibiscus flower on top of the dresser (he'll come inside there when the fumigation truck goes by, I think). I sit down to see whether the lizard, who also hides and tricks me, will survive these fabrications: clouds of smoke and salvation for beings who attempt to have their doubles, their ghosts.

Perhaps my father will return through the reflection of the water in a plastic bucket, the one we set under leaks in the roof. Or he'll hide in the dregs of adulterated coffee, or get in through other "scaffoldings of desire" (bad metaphor), traversing the distance that has spanned thirty-six years, thousands of syllables of incomprehension, fights, and impossible substitutions for some simultaneous match chess championship that never took place (with elegance or without it), and where there won't be any winners.

Nose and cheek, dark-skinned. Little papers left over from my birthday presents, stored in Chinese boxes with their nostalgic pyramid shapes and hand-painted palaces I never visited. Taffeta ribbons tearing before my eyes, kept in a drawer of the antique chest. Sticky labels from his shirts (still with the invisible mark of kisses from the other women, their lipstick). These are nothing more than bad metaphors for a father, ridiculous wrappings around the act of surviving him. But something important was left for me, the best thing, which taught me to be impressionistic from that point forward: this corner, also called the Corner of Sin, from which I still contemplate him in the wrong place—on someone else's countenance.

The store disappeared, taking its display windows, its fragile Italian dolls, and the special-order departments that sold illusions, articles, and curiosities, including Casino socks I bought for him to wear at my fifteenth birthday celebration (socks he never got to put on). I may wander off or get distracted, but I did ride behind that goat, who continues to follow the same circuit through the scenery in this park, pulling her simple cart alongside a younger animal; I go on sitting here in order to shore up everything that my childhood once was. Remains of an art deco building (its walls well worn), the luxury of thinking that because I stay right here, looking at it, its cracked base will fall onto the page if I come back again and the building is gone.

Then my father said: "Always come back here together after I'm gone…" and that was the last time we visited Santa Fe. To be able to hold onto something, it was necessary for an order to the contrary to be given.

I was so happy when he would play the silvery grater (the one in our family photo), which an old man left for me. It made a sound like an empty, shiny seashell! Can I retrieve that sound by scraping at the text

cia? ¿Dónde se mantuvieron ocultas y por qué se mantuvieron ajenas al trasteo? Así, como protuberancias o bultos que de pronto enfilan por una bocacalle, en la oscuridad, los poemas estaban allí, configurados y anteriores al acto. "Desdibujo de recuerdos"—diría—, fragmentos de botellas ambarinas; pedazos de metrallas; restos de conversaciones (esas palabras que se desprenden de su panorama y regresan con capital reciclado a un ajuste de cuentas al pasado).

Si reaparecen, son la barrera de coral que impulsa al movimiento subsiguiente... "He saltado sobre esta cordillera, aquellos arrecifes, el muro de cemento gris del parque, tengo que bucear o escalar lo más hondo de esa altura que se impone contra el tiempo"—nos dicen las estrellas.

Después, he nadado hacia los arrecifes prometidos confundiendo un tono verde petróleo que es el color de cierta zona de mi mente. Cuando pegaba en las libretas escolares una fotografía, esta tenía el color que exploraba, pero no me zambullí jamás en él. Busqué todas las fugas posibles para no restablecer ese color, su densidad de lugar prohibido en unos ojos. Marca de agua, inútil geografía de una costa perdida que me dejó mi madre. Por eso, saco piedras erradas, de aquí y de allá. Trasteo ese fondo pegajoso entre otros paisajes, pero no me atrevo a entrar a ninguno. La prohibición es absoluta. "... Si los paisajes se vendieran—dice R.L. Stevenson en *Travels with a Donkey*— como los recortables de mi niñez, a un penique en blanco y negro y a dos peniques con color, estaría toda mi vida gastando dos peniques cada día..."

Por dos peniques cada día he recorrido otras costas que, aparentemente, cambiarían la flecha lanzada, pero tampoco lo logré. No fue así. Al final, las libretas escolares con láminas recortadas, sin mucha precisión (esos recortables de otros mares, otros ojos), me niegan la travesía que no hice. Me sumergí, pero sólo en una sustancia olvido que logra la única permanencia al volver. Siempre, claro, por rutas que nos mortifican y de las que no salimos ilesos nunca sin perder dominio de la sensación sobre ellas. Aguas malas donde quedó el poema, con su mancha de salitre, intacto: esa materia gelatinosa donde quedamos abrazados mi padre y yo. Fue mi venganza contra su pérdida, lo sé, sostener ese olvido monstruoso. Entrar por el pisapapel (burbuja de fantasía, ya no hay cristal) donde estaremos volteados para siempre en tono más turbio y hasta ridículo, para recuperar cualquier cambio. "Por eso estoy aquí"— grito, sujeta a la profundidad donde me dejó.

with a stone from a fallen building? These things now returning intermittently: why did they go away? Where were they hidden, and why did they remain alien through the move? Like that, like protuberances or shapes suddenly making their entrance onto a street, in the dark, the poems were there, already configured, prior to the act. "Blurring of memories,"— I would say—, fragments of amberina bottles; shrapnel; remains of conversations (those words that emerge out of their panorama and return with capital to be recycled in the settling of scores with the past).

If they reappear, they're the barrier reef, which impels the subsequent motion ... "I leapt over this mountain range, those reefs, the gray cement wall at the park, I have to swim under or scale the most extensive distance that prevails against time," the stars say to us.

Later, I've swum out toward those promised reefs in a state of confusion about an oil-green tone, the color of a certain zone inside my mind. When I pasted a photo onto my notebooks, it held the color I was exploring, but I never dove down into it. I sought all possible escapes for not re-establishing that color, with its density of a prohibited location in someone else's eyes. Watermark, useless geography of a lost coastline that my mother left to me. So I take up rocks displaced from here, from there. I move the sticky background color around among other landscapes, but I don't dare enter any of them. The prohibition is absolute. "If landcapes were sold," says R.L. Stevenson in *Travels with a Donkey*, "like the sheets of characters of my childhood, one penny plain and twopence coloured, I should go the length of twopence every day of my life..."

For twopence every day I've gone the length of other coasts, which seemed like it could change the arrow's flight, but I didn't succeed that way either. It wasn't like that. In the end the school notebooks, their sheets cut with little regularity or precision (those sheets of characters for other oceans, other eyes) deny me that crossing, the one I didn't make. I dove in, but just into a substance of oblivion, which acquires its only permanence upon arrival. Always, of course, by routes that cause us great pain, and from which we never walk away unharmed without losing control over the sensations they create. Dangerous waters where the poem remained intact, with its salt stain: a gelatinous medium in which my father and I are embraced. Sustaining a monstrous forgetfulness was my revenge against his loss, I know. Entering a paperweight (a bubble of fantasy, there's no crystal any more) where we'll always be revolving inside a color, one ever more murky, and even more absurd, as we hope to recall the change. "That's why I'm here," I cry, settled into the depth where he left me.

El diablo

Había leído *Cartas del verano de 1926* escritas entre Marina Tsvietáieva, Rainer María Rilke y Boris Pasternak, y había sentido, entre el tapiz creado por el destino de aquellos dos hombres y esta mujer, la fuerza que los aprisionaba—donde el sentido de progreso no estaba en la acumulación de una acción tras otra para llegar a un fin, sino en las propias teclas que ella ya hacía sonar desde entonces, porque "era posible ir con ellas como por una escalera"—y ese sería el único sentido de su progresión triangular. "Porque esa escalera estaba debajo de sus manos", apretando un dolor sostenido bajo la cuerda, entre ella, el martinete y la nota, por la pérdida de un sentido que ellos (los tres poetas de aquellas cartas) se provocaron entre sí; sentido indescifrable para el hombre contemporáneo tan necesitado de acciones concretas, de veracidad, y de hechos. Por la imposibilidad de una vida realizada en la vida (la vida realizada cual escala cromática de Marina), pasé a un sentimiento intemporal, algo así, como la nostalgia de no poseer aquel espíritu que está prisionero para siempre en la palabra, donde uno "se defiende entero o es aniquilado por entero"—como dijera la Tsvietáieva, y como pasó también con su vida.

Por eso, no hay géneros entre los libros recopilados más tarde, por su editora y traductora del ruso Selma Ancira: hay extensiones, o silencios, seudópodos para vivir dentro de un interminable arpegio. El género es la vida.

Ahora, con *El diablo*, de Marina Tsvietáieva (1892–1941), publicado por Anagrama, he tenido la posibilidad de tocar otra vez, las fibras de esta poeta que, venida del "más allá", del absoluto de la metáfora de su creencia en ella, entre la guerra, la miseria, el desalojo, la barbarie, la presión y la muerte de sus seres más queridos en el vórtice del siglo y del stalinismo, coloca la tecla de nuevo sobre una prosa de tal intensidad—segmentos sesgados de una vida; diásporas de su imposibilidad de vivir—que se pueden apretar y sostener todavía entre los dedos.

No es una lectura común la que hacemos con este libro; tampoco es una lectura que se puede reiterar: es una lectura muy especial, extraña. ¿Biografía? ¿Paisajes? ¿Sueños? Más bien gestos continuos; conceptos emotivos; conceptos que sienten por los gestos. Como si el libro se quejara, palpitara, y saliera de su forma convencional de libro donde se encierra entre páginas, y estalla. Devolviéndonos en imágenes, duras, frías, cortantes, hasta el colmo de esa profundidad frágil de las cosas aparentes, y a través de disímiles jerarquías superpuestas de lenguajes,

The Devil

I once read *Letters: Summer 1926*, composed between Marina Tsvetaeva, Rainer Maria Rilke, and Boris Pasternak. Throughout this tapestry, the destination of two particular men and this one woman, I felt the power that held them prisoner. There the sense of progression was found not through the accumulation of one action after another, arriving at some end, but on the very keyboards she was already playing at that time, because "it was possible to move along them as if along a stairway"—and this would be the only meaning of their triangular progression. "Because that stairway was underneath her hands," pressing on a prolonged ache under the string, between her, the hammer, and the note, through the loss of meaning that they (the three poets from those letters) prompted in each other: a meaning indecipherable to contemporary man, so needful of concrete actions, veracity, and facts. Through the inability to realize a life within life (life realized as Marina's chromatic scale), I moved toward a feeling of timelessness, something like that. Like the nostalgia created by not possessing the spirit eternally imprisoned in the word, where one "defends oneself utterly or is annihilated utterly"—as Tsvetaeva would say, and as she lived her life.

This is why genres don't exist within the books compiled later by Selma Ancira, her editor and translator from the Russian: there are extensions, or silences, pseudopodia for living within a never-ending arpeggio. Life is the genre.

Now, with *El diablo* (*The Devil*), a collection by Marina Tsvietaieva (1892–1941) released by Anagram, I've had another opportunity to test the fibers of this poet. Coming from the "beyond," from the absoluteness of metaphor and her belief in it; coming through war, misery, eviction, barbarism, duress and the death of the people she most loved, in the vortex of the century and Stalinism, this poet presses her keys down once more on a prose of such intensity—slanted segments of a life, diasporas cut from her impossibility for living—that they can still be touched, held up between your fingers.

It's not an ordinary form of reading that we do with this book, nor is it a reading that can be paraphrased: it's a very special kind of reading, a strange one. Biography? Landscapes? Dreams? More like ongoing gestures, emotional concepts, concepts that signify through gestures. As if the book groans, throbs, and exits the conventional book form enclosed between its pages, blowing up. Returning to us in images—hard, cold, sharp—until it reaches the peak of fragile profundity found in visible things; returning to us through unmatched, superimposed hierarchies

la unidad rota de la utopía, quebrada y partida de un ser, lúcido, preciso, atormentado, que se rompe como un vidrio en mil pedazos. Para colocar luego, en algún sitio—en ese sitio donde el caleidoscopio se recompone únicamente con el tacto de la memoria—eso que bien puede llamarse un alma, un peso específico de algo, una iluminación del proceso (o de los procesos continuados y repetidos a perpetuidad) que la hicieron sobrevivir, dentro de aquella densidad de material y sustancia fría, congelada que, desde su infancia, ella recogió con esas partículas de polvo de expresión únicas e irreversibles.

Marina nos muestra, como una niña, con extrema naturalidad y sencillez, cómo las colocó luego en las márgenes de una escritura a la vez continua y fragmentada; entre el orden perfecto de los desórdenes de sus referencias; de los andamios que se sintetizan luego en una negativa rotunda de alma—como la oscilación negativa del péndulo de un reloj desde atrás hacia delante—, que escoge al diablo—ella escoge al diablo; Marina, la niña, siempre escoge al diablo; Marina, la poeta, escoge al diablo; Marina la mujer y la madre, escoge al diablo—para reafirmar su "no ser", la imposibilidad de su contrario, para provocar y sostener, si fuera posible, algún dios con la fuerza biunívoca del mal.

El piano abre la boca y enseña sus dientes: la palabra muerde (a su madre que se muere sobre el piano, doblegada; al abuelo real y ficcionado; tira la cajita de dados con Asia, su hermana más pequeña, juega a la infancia, y se abre también a la pregunta, de cuclillas bajo el piano, sobre la muerte que se aproxima sin respuesta; las cubre un terciopelo marrón). Siempre la distancia que faltaba entre ella y el obstáculo de su deseo real la alcanza con sus dedos largos, inconclusos. Se abraza al piano, y lo que está detrás de la música es un lamento que escuchamos todavía, como si la escala fuera reinvertida cronológicamente en el tiempo sentido por su visión de la escritura. La muerte de su infancia y de su madre. Los dados no fallan, amarillentos también entre sus dedos, como notas, como páginas…

Esto no es un libro, tampoco un acorde, tampoco una vida. Es una violencia. Una violación de los sentidos. Nos enseña algo: quien está dentro de nosotros, trasteándonos, para marcarnos con su marca secreta cuando estamos desprevenidos, es el miedo… "Dios es para mí, el miedo", asegura. Porque del miedo salen estas cosas, cosas del diablo, caras.

of language, the broken unity of utopia, cracked and split off an existence that is lucid, precise, tormented, and breaks like a windowpane into a thousand pieces. Then, in the place where the kaleidoscope takes new form with the sensation of a memory, it locates that which could well be called a soul, a specific weight of some thing, an enlightenment about the process (or ongoing processes, repeated in perpetuity). Something that allowed her to survive within that material's density, and its cold, frozen substance she had been collecting since childhood with particles of dust, expressions both unique and irreversible.

Marina shows us, with a child's great naturalness and simplicity, how she placed her particles into the margins of a writing at once continuous and fragmented; into the perfect order of the disorders of her references; of the scaffoldings that synthesize into a categorical negation of the soul—like the negative oscillation of the clock pendulum, from back to front—which chooses the devil—she chooses the devil; Marina, the girl, always chooses the devil; Marina, the poet, chooses the devil; Marina the woman and the mother chooses the devil—in order to reaffirm her "not-existence," the impossibility of her opposite, in order to prod and hold up, if it were possible, some god with the one-to-one power of evil.

The piano opens its mouth and shows its teeth: the word bites (her mother, crushed, dying in the piano; the real and fictional grandfather; she throws the box of dice with Asia, her youngest sister, playing at childhood—and opens herself to the question, crouching under the piano, about the death approaching without an answer; she covers them in brown velvet). She always catches the distance between her and the obstacle of her real desire, with her long inconclusive fingers. She hugs herself to the piano, and the thing behind the music is a lament we continue to hear, as if the scale were chronologically reinvested into a tempo, sensed through her vision of writing. The death of her childhood and her mother. The dice don't falter, yellowed between her fingers like notes, like pages...

This is not a book, nor is it a chord, or a life. It's violence. The violation of the senses. It teaches us something: that the presence inside us, moving around, marking us with a secret sign when our guard drops, is fear... "God, to me, is fear," she states firmly. Because these things emerging out of the fear, the devil's faces, cost far too much.

La zanja

Lo primero que vi fue aquella zanja donde unos hombres con camisetas azules de trabajo, rompían la tierra compacta para hallar unas tuberías. Después, Plácido me llevó en su "psicorre" destartalado. Recuerdo el camino hacia la casa, a través de la línea del mar que se quebró contra la tendedera de los vecinos de enfrente, donde colgaban unos trapos negros. Parecía una ropa muy usada, sayas amplias, corpiños, telas enormes lanzadas sobre los cordeles.

Desde la ventana, mi mirada localizó hacia la derecha todo el recorrido y el paisaje cambió del azul profundo al negro prieto. Ella lloraba en el cuarto contiguo con su chemise de fingido piqué blanco, muy estrecho cerca de las rodillas. Estaba acurrucada en una esquina de la cama. En su cara encontraba una respuesta definitiva a mi pronta venida, a mi interrupción, a mi apuro.

—Ha muerto —me dijo, y siguió enroscando el dobladillo de falso piqué.

Entraron en tropel algunos muchachos de la universidad y el rector. Nunca lo había visto antes.

—Fue el mejor alumno de todo el curso. No había dos como él.

Mi bata de "guinga" verde y blanca, refractaba cuadritos regulares contra sus espejuelos. Cada vez, me apretaba más el hueco, con un fruncido disimulado con encaje. No lloré. Lo sabía. Siempre lo sospeché, por la zanja abierta esa mañana en el Vedado. Tenía el pelo muy sucio y me lo recogía con un pañuelo de tela dura, con una cotorra al frente que en cualquier otro momento hubiera parecido simpática.

Ella había llegado, seca, sin sangre. Lo sospeché desde aquella conversación con él, en la ventana, por donde ahora veía la interminable tendedera de cordeles de alambre mohosos con ropajes negros y enfilados hacia mí.

—Era mi hermano. El mejor estudiante.

Sus ojos estaban confundidos por el golpe. El golpe fue primero. Descarriló de pronto su conciencia, y rompió la causalidad.

—Subrutinas, me dijo, obsesionado.

Todo se desmanteló desde aquella mañana. La tapa de la caja era de una madera grisácea y parecía dispuesta a estallar. Pero no se abrió más.

Me quedé rezagada en un banco recordando todos los momentos en que le había negado un sacapuntas, la tijerita de recortar papel, los espejuelos calobares. Misceláneas. La muerte es un recordatorio ejemplar

The Grave

The first one I saw was the ditch where some men in blue work t-shirts were breaking compacted ground in search of piping. Afterwards, Plácido took me in his rickety pickup. I remember the way to the house, along the line of ocean that broke against the clothesline at the neighbors' home across the street, where pieces of black cloth hung. It looked like very used clothing, broad skirts, brassieres, large strips of fabric thrown over the lines.

From the window my gaze traced the whole route, moving toward the right, and the landscape changed from deep blue to dense black. She was crying in the next room in her chemise made of imitation white piqué, very tight around the knees. She was curled up in a corner of the bed. In her face I found a definitive answer to my sudden arrival, my interruption, my haste.

"He died," she told me, and kept on twisting the false piqué hem.

Some boys from the university and the rector crowded in. I had never seen him before.

"He was the best student in his entire class. No one else like him."

My green and white gingham robe refracted against her spectacles in steady little squares. The hollow pressed more and more tightly against me with a hidden gathering of lace. I didn't cry. I knew. Had always suspected, by the open ditch that morning in the Vedado district. My hair was filthy and I wore it tied up in a kerchief of coarse cloth, with a parrot on the front who would have looked happy at any other moment.

She arrived dry and bloodless. I had suspected it since that conversation with him, at the window, through which I now saw the interminable clothesline, its rusty wire lines with black robes in rows aimed at me.

"He was my brother. The best student."

Her eyes were confused from the blow. The blow came first. It abruptly derailed consciousness, smashed causality.

"Subroutines," she told me. "He was obsessed."

Everything fell apart after that morning. The lid to the box was made out of gray wood and seemed as though it were about to blow up. But it never opened again.

I stayed behind on a bench, remembering all the moments when I refused him a pencil sharpener, the little pair of scissors for trimming paper, the calobar glasses. Miscellaneous things. Death is an

de nuestras mezquindades. El encaje cuadrado había perdido su forma bajo mis dientes, lo mordía, lo destrozaba.

Los empleados del acueducto, supongo, cerraban la zanja. El aguá corría de nuevo por las tuberías hacia el tabique de mi nariz, sobre el puente de los espejuelos y mojaba también el pelo sucio y cuarteado. Ni aquella noche ni la siguiente, quitaron los vestidos prietos del alambre a la distancia donde mi madre y yo, nos acurrucábamos de espaldas a la visión del cordel. Ella enrollaba su dobladillo, yo, mi escote. Pasaría un día, un mes, un año, y hasta una veintena más. La premonición del diente enfermo y caído sobre el hueco de la palma de mi mano, no sirvió tampoco para asegurar las cosas de la familia.

El niño nació pocos días después, de nalgas, con un pelo rubio y rizado.

Era mi hijo. Me costó encontrarle un nombre que lo identificara.

Toqué el borde del vaso, pero no tomé aquella leche espumosa que me habían servido después del parto. Dentro de las líneas de un recorrido siempre hay una provocación que espera empatarse. Había sobrevivido quince días más, y ella, la señora que viene y nos sirve la leche, la que nos provoca cavando con sonido reiterado, en la zanja, me había permitido desdoblarme por un rato.

Había por todas partes encaje blanco y toda la ropa tendida (pañales, blusas, mantas, camisoncitos) estaba tan pulcra como el recién nacido.

—Mi hijo se hace santo, lo malo es cuando algo no se puede restañar.

No encuentro frases que sirvan de resignación.

Así como se fue el hermano, llegó el hijo.

—¿Será la sucesión la única restauración?—pregunto, sin obtener respuesta.

Sólo, cuando no se puede suceder, pensé, viene ella, y al fin, te agarra.

La tendedera ha quedado vacía. Dos o tres alambres sostenidos por un fondo de cielo y abismo. No se confunde más la línea del mar con nada.

exemplary reminder of our meanness. The squared lace lost its shape under my teeth—I was biting it, destroying it.

I assume the employees at the aqueduct filled their ditch. The water running again through the pipes toward the septum in my nose, over the bridge of the spectacles, over my dirty, splitting hair. Not that night, nor the next, did they take the dark clothing down from the wires so far away from the place where my mother and I were curled up, our backs to the sight of the cords. She was rolling her hem, I my neckline. A day would go by, a month, a year, and up to twenty more. The premonition of an infected tooth falling onto the hollow in the palm of my hand did nothing, either, to make family affairs more certain.

The boy was born a few days later, rump first, with curly blond hair.

He was my son. I had a hard time finding a name to identify him.

I touched the edge of the glass but didn't drink the foamy milk they served me after the delivery. Between lines of a route there's always a provocation ready to tie the lines and balance them out. I had survived fifteen more days, and she—as a lady who comes and serves us milk, milk that provokes us by gnawing at the grave with a repetitive sound— allowed me to split in two for a little while.

White lace was everywhere and all the clothes hanging outside (baby clothes, blouses, blankets, nighties) were clean as the newborn boy.

"My son becomes a saint. The bad part is when something can't be staunched."

I can't find sentences appropriate for resignation.

As the brother left, so the son arrived.

"Is succession the only form of restoration?" I ask, without receiving any answer.

But when it can't happen, I thought, she comes, and in the end she gets you.

The clothesline has been cleared. Two or three wires suspended against a backdrop of sky and abyss. The line of the ocean no longer merges with anything else.

Una muchacha llevó las primeras flores

He leído, mientras llueve y el aire recicla la humedad en las viejas paredes del edificio, el entierro de Alexandr A. Blok contado por Nina Berberova en su autobiografía. He visto el Neva, las calles desiertas de Leningrado, el fusilamiento de Gumilov y de aquellos otros. El funeral tuvo lugar un día 10 de agosto, un poco después, el fusilamiento del marido de Ajmátova, y todavía oigo recitar aquellos versos suyos, montados unos encima de otros, como el traqueteo del féretro en su larga caja, al centro, entre los caballos que avanzan con muchos versos ritmados. "El lugar se hallaba desierto y en calma . . ."—dice la Berberova. El lugar sigue intacto, sólo unas flores secas que antes fueron blancas azucenas, cuatro para mayor exactitud, con largos tallos cortados por una muchacha que ya tampoco existe, están junto a mi mesa de trabajo esta mañana.

Uno es de lugares remotos. Lugares de los que se apropia por algo que no sabría definir. Yo supe que también estaba allí, en el fin de una época, mientras las viejitas rusas (crédulas) rezaban y seguían oficiando por no perder la costumbre de pedir. Nina iba con un vestido hecho con una cortina, tal vez blanca, y los puños cerrados eran del terciopelo rojizo de una alfombra muy usada. Esto es lo que tengo, un recuerdo que llega como una postal mutilada, un olor a incienso que se mueve en el incensario que lleva ante la comitiva, el viejo sacerdote hasta el cementerio de Smolensk. ¿Cómo se siente la muerte de un poeta y los poemas esperados que ya no llegarán?

He visto, "con los ojos abiertos," como quien mira una línea tras otra, con ritmo creciente que empieza y no se pierde en la isla Vasili cuando cierro los ojos y el libro. ¿Qué importancia tiene para alguien estar o no haber estado? Pero los versos de Alexandr A. Blok resisten, cortantes, el paso de su féretro y el fusilamiento de tantos. Están en una mañana tan cercana y lejana. Cuando pienso en la muerte del poeta y en su poesía, siento los mismos espasmos que ella sintió entonces, aquella muchacha que pretendía escribir. Algo que no se comprende nunca, que no conlleva una queja, diría, sólo una sensación de que las cosas serán contadas de otra forma, con otra disposición, ya que cada poeta se lleva una manera de contar, única. ¿Versos? ¿Estrofas? ¿Principios? ¿Repeticiones? ¿Finales? Sus palabras serán explicadas o dadas a otros del círculo en la mesa, donde cada uno querría ser una voz.

A Young Woman Brought the First Flowers

As it rains and the air recirculates the humidity on the aged walls of the building, I read about the burial of Alexandr Blok, which Nina Berberova recounts in her autobiography. I've seen the Neva, the deserted streets of Leningrad, the shooting of Gumilev and the other men. The funeral took place on the tenth of August; not long afterwards came the shooting of Akhmatova's husband; and I can still hear the recitation of her lines, some piled on top of others, like the rattling of the casket in its long box, in the center, between the horses moving forward with many rhymed verses. "The location was deserted and quiet," says Berberova. The place is intact. Just a few dried flowers that used to be white lilies, four of them to be more exact, with long stems cut by a young woman who no longer exists either: they're next to my work table this morning.

One is from places far away. Places appropriate for something I wouldn't know how to define. I found out that she was there too, at the end of an era, as the elderly Russian ladies (credulous) prayed and kept on observing their rituals, so as not to lose the custom of petitioning. Nina was wearing a dress made from a curtain, maybe a white one, and her clenched fists were covered in reddish velvet taken from an old swatch of carpet. This is what I have, a memory that arrives like a mutilated postcard, the scent of incense moving through the burner, carried by the aged priest leading the procession to the Smolensk cemetery. How does the death of a poet feel, the death of poems anticipated but never to arrive?

I've seen it, my "eyes wide open," as one who reads from one line to the next, a rhythm building, one that starts up and doesn't disappear into Vasilyevsky Island, when I close my eyes and the book. What does it matter for anyone to have been there or not? But the verses by Alexandr A. Blok—cutting—withstand the passing of his casket and the execution of so many people. They are there, in a tomorrow both near and far away. When I think about the death of the poet, and about his poetry, I feel the spasms she felt, then, that young woman who was trying to write. Something you never understand, which does not involve complaint, I'd say, just a sensation that things will be told in a different way, with a different arrangement, since every poet is guided by a unique way of telling. Verses? Stanzas? Beginnings? Repetitions? Endings? Their words will be explained or given to others in the circle around the table, where each one would like to be a voice.

I

"Durante varias semanas vivimos en un silencio total…" La voz se había perdido. Había, entonces, y todavía lo hay, un entumecimiento. Era verano, pero no como aquí en la Habana, vendría un otoño real. Otro poeta de una isla que no era Vasili ni estaba junto al Neva también ha muerto lejos. No pudo regresar, no regresó. Otra manera de fusilamiento, no dejar regresar a los poetas, a sus almas. La muerte no tiene permiso de salida o de entrada. Llega y desplaza cualquier petición, aunque las viejitas sigan oficiando renuentes a comprender que los poderes quieren destruir la razón de las cosas que se sienten, tan torpes y extrañas, mientras se comen pasteles de una mala harina cuarteándose en la boca, y se toma un té reciclado.

No dejemos que los tallos se quiebren. No dejemos que la muerte de un poeta ocurra en un aula, donde él esté tan solo junto a extraños. Recojamos al corazón que ha pretendido ser más intenso. Que el ritmo siga balanceando su féretro como si fuera una ola, ese movimiento de lenguajes dispersos con los que soñó un retorno. Los poetas también van al cielo o al infierno si los desplazamos de su lugar de ser. Sé que es una petición romántica, un deseo frustrado e ingenuo a estas alturas.

Él murió en un aula fría del norte y no pudimos tenderle una manta, un caparazón. Blok, Gumilov, Ajmátova, Marina, Heberto, y tantos otros entierros que no presencié. Sólo "un canto melodioso y vibrante mientras se llevaban el cuerpo del difunto . . ." Un canto de niños en una iglesia destartalada y local. Una pobrísima ceremonia. Nosotros desnudos y con las cabezas cubiertas, a diferencia de aquellos, hacia algún perdido cementerio también local, esperando el turno de cada poeta muerto que ha llegado hasta aquí sin permiso de entrada.

Demasiada pretensión esa de un espacio para enterrar a un poeta. De encontrar cosas que no todos comprenden con facilidad. Lugares, sitios, recodos. Un poeta está enterrado entre palabras desde mucho antes de haber muerto. Recoge las sobras de las sensaciones, sus esquirlas, para recomponerlas. Ninguna distancia entre épocas, ni velocidad que opaquen el traquetear del carro, los caballos de entonces. Ha muerto un poeta, y luego, otro. Siempre la misma rutina de morir inconclusa, en la mitad o la periferia de algo.

No sabemos cuáles fueron sus obsesiones. Sabemos de textos intermediarios, arrítmicos, como trámites. No podemos sacar cuentas de cuántos minutos estuvo frente al papel planeando llegar, vivir, morir enteramente en una imagen. Cuánto alargó cada segundo de volver y de pedir amparo en su muerte. Cada instante, en que contar cuesta en verdad un poco, un fusilamiento, una negación, un fin, un céntimo.

I

"For several weeks we lived in total silence…" The voice has been lost. There was, then, and still is, numbness. It was summer, but not like here in Havana; a true autumn would come. Another poet from an island that was not the Vasilyevsky, was not along the Neva, has also died far away. He couldn't return, didn't return. Another type of execution, this matter of not allowing poets, their souls, to return. Death has no permit for exits or entrances. It arrives and displaces all petitions, even if the elderly ladies continue to officiate, unwilling to understand that powers want to destroy the truth of things they feel, so slow-moving and strange, as they eat pastries made with bad flour, spoiling in their mouths, and drink tea made from reused bags.

Let's not allow the stems to break. Let's not allow the death of a poet to happen in a lecture room, where he may be alone with strangers. Let's gather up the heart that tried to be more passionate. So the rhythm will continue to balance his casket as if it were a wave, that movement of scattered languages with which he dreamed return. Poets also go to heaven or hell if we displace them from their place of existence. I know it's a romantic request, a desire both frustrated and naïve at this point.

He died in a cold classroom to the north and we couldn't lay a blanket or oilcloth over him. Blok, Gumilev, Akhmatova, Marina, Heberto, and so many other burials I didn't attend. Just "a melodious and rolling chant as they carried the body of the deceased." The song of children in a dilapidated local church. An extraordinarily modest ceremony. Naked and with our heads covered, we, by contrast to them, move toward some lost cemetery that is also local, awaiting the turn of every dead poet who has come this far without an entry permit.

Too much pretense, this business about a burial plot for a poet. About finding things that not everyone will understand easily. Places, sites, bends. A poet is buried in words long before dying. He gathers leftover sensations, his splinters, to repair them. No distance between eras, or velocity, to dull the rattling of the car, the horses from that time. One poet has died, and then another. Always the same routine for dying: unfinished, halfway through or at the periphery of something.

We don't know what his obsessions were. We know about texts that are intermediary, arrhythmic, like procedures. We can't calculate how many minutes he spent facing the paper, planning to arrive, live, die entirely inside an image. How long each second extended for returning and requesting shelter in his death. Each instant in which telling really costs a little something, a shooting, a negation, an end, a cent. Let's not

¡No dejemos morir sin asilo a los poetas! Traerlos al sitio seguro de las cuatro azucenas, de esas flores blancas que una muchacha desconocida depositó anticipándose al horror que vendría después de la congelación. No dejarlo en el destierro, en el desamparo.

No teníamos idea de si éramos los más dotados, o si ellos serían los más dotados, entonces. Empujábamos el carro, cuyas ruedas crujían en mitad de una carretera llena de huecos, de baches y desperdicios. Llevábamos un cuerpo errante que desde el siglo pasado, y del otro, seguía conservándose. El cuerpo no tenía señas visibles de pertenencia al tiempo ni al país, tampoco. Era un cuerpo común, recuperado. Junto al cuerpo, un cartón forrado con un hule negro y unas cuantas iniciales que indicaban un nombre, traían sus últimos poemas presillados todavía con cierta vanidad. La llovizna de aquel día los mojaba y el viento ligero los batía. No se trataba de versificaciones o de poesía antigua o contemporánea, de parnasianos, modernistas o surrealistas, se trataba del cuerpo del poeta que llegaba con sus manuscritos como si fueran la misma cosa.

II

Al abrir el correo, muy temprano, tenía en él la noticia en una sola línea, enviada por Francisco Morán desde Arlington: "… Heberto murió…"

Conocí a Heberto Padilla en 1994, en Estocolmo, durante un encuentro de escritores "de adentro" y "de afuera" de la Isla, en un hotel donde hasta los espejos reflejaban una gran paranoia. Entre cenas con lenguados, tambores de papas, carne de venado gris, manzanas y vinos, coincidimos. Él, todo el tiempo haciendo chistes, enamorándose cada vez más de la vida y de la poeta cubana Lourdes Gil, me demostró cómo la lejanía y las circunstancias extraliterarias pueden desfigurar una imagen. Fui rompiendo el estereotipo que me habían dado hasta recomponer a este poeta de humor político, tan jaranero. Lo que había constituido un martirio para mí, volar tan lejos sin saber bien por qué ni para qué, tuvo un sentido: esa amistad que nació entre cisnes y fotos congeladas con las noches blancas del Báltico como telón de fondo.

Cuando nos volvimos a encontrar, ese mismo año en Madrid, en el encuentro "La isla entera", él había usado para su ponencia, fragmentos de autores jóvenes que le había dado en Estocolmo y que eran desconocidos, por entonces, en el exilio. En ese encuentro de Madrid me dejó una edición de su poesía, en un libro blanco de tapa dura.

En 1998 estuve en la universidad de Princeton y Lourdes Gil y él, fueron a visitarme a casa de un amigo de la infancia que vivía en New

allow poets to die without sanctuary! Bring them to that safe place with four lilies, those white flowers that an unknown girl left, anticipating the horror to come after the freeze. Don't leave him in exile, abandoned.

We didn't know whether we were the most gifted, or whether they would be the most gifted, at that time. We pushed the cart whose wheels creaked down the middle of a road, one full of holes, badly filled potholes and waste. We bore a wandering body from the former century, and another one, still preserved. The body had no visible signs of belonging to the moment, or to the nation either. It was an ordinary body, rescued. Next to the body, a box lined with a black oilcloth and a few initials indicating a name: they carried his final poems stapled together, still with a certain vanity. The drizzle from that day got them wet and the light breeze whipped them around. It wasn't about versifications, or poetry that was ancient or contemporary, or about Parnassians, Modernists or Surrealists; it was about the body of the poet who arrived with his manuscripts as if they were one and the same thing.

II

When I opened the email, very early, it contained the news in one single line sent by Francisco Morán from Arlington: "Heberto died."

I met Heberto Padilla in 1994, in Stockholm, during a conference of writers "from outside" and "from inside" the island, at a hotel where even the mirrors flashed with paranoia. Between dinners with tongue, drums of potatoes, venison from gray deer, apples and wine, we met by chance. He, always making jokes, falling ever more in love with life and with the Cuban poet Lourdes Gil, showed me how distance and extra-literary circumstances can distort an image. I was breaking through the stereotype they had given me, recreating this poet with his political humor and such an appetite for celebration. Something that had constituted martyrdom for me, flying so far away without knowing really how or why, took on meaning: the friendship born between swans and photographs, frozen with white Baltic nights as their backdrop.

When we met again that same year in Madrid at another conference, called "The Whole Island," he used excerpts from the young poets whose work I had given him in Stockholm, then unknown in exile, for his talk. At that Madrid conference he left me his poetry in a white hardback edition.

In 1998 when I was at Princeton University, he and Lourdes Gil came to visit me at the house of a childhood friend living in New Jersey. They brought me a cream-colored, embroidered silk blouse as a

Jersey. Me llevaban una blusa crema de seda bordada como regalo. Una de esas blusas de señoras que se vendían en las ferias chinas y eran caras. Nos tiramos fotos que no conservo, porque se quedaron en la cámara de mi amigo. Fue la última vez que lo vi.

Luego, en febrero del 2000 conversamos por teléfono. Él partía ese mismo día para sus clases en Filadelfia creo, y yo estaba en N.Y., así que no pudimos vernos. Durante esta conversación, me insistió en su deseo de visitar la isla, en ese trámite que inicié desde que me lo pidiera unos años antes. Me dijo que ninguna otra consideración "que no fuera el deseo que él tenía de venir a la isla, era importante ya", y sentí un llanto del otro lado del teléfono. Un tanto seco.

Unas semanas antes de su muerte, Armando Suárez Cobián, me enviaba por correo electrónico desde N.Y., la petición de Lourdes Gil, de que Heberto no estaba bien de salud y quería venir. Volví a los pasillos, a pedir que Heberto insistía en venir. Alguien me respondió que "haría todo lo que estaba a su alcance para que así fuera, y que traería a Heberto".

Si la cultura sirve para intermediar con el poder, debe responder a esta petición y traer a un poeta exiliado y enfermo a su tierra natal, para despedirse.

Por eso hago este recuento. Es una deuda. No sé por qué ahora, no sé por qué en noviembre. Todo esto lo recordé mientras Nina Berberova contaba la muerte de Alexandr A. Blok y tuve que cerrar su libro. Hubo en nuestra fugaz amistad, más de lo que pudimos expresarnos por la distancia y la paranoia. No tengo ninguna intención de rescatarla con otros adornos, así fue. Unas cuantas fotos, unos abrazos fraternales y una pieza que bailamos como despedida. No quiero tampoco extrapolar lo que no pudo ser. Tengo una "gestión" que hacer por los poetas muertos.

Heberto Padilla entró sin permiso a su tierra natal que fue siempre la página. Entró a su página definitiva. Para mí, que lo escuché recitar sus poemas, decir sus chistes llenos de humor político, que pude oír su voz por última vez del otro lado del teléfono (ese otro lado contra cualquier razonamiento injusto que no lo dejó regresar y tenerlo de tan lejano, cerca), sigue aquí, de donde nunca se fue, a donde ya regresó.

III

No hubiera querido perder nunca ese silencio de su voz del otro lado del teléfono. Pero vivimos, porque podemos olvidar. Cuando lo escribo, siento que pierdo esos fragmentos de conversación, esa cadencia que

gift. One of those women's blouses sold at Chinese fairs, very expensive. We took photos, which I don't have because they were on my friend's camera. It was the last time I saw him.

Next we spoke by phone in February 2000. He was leaving that same day to teach classes in, I think, Philadelphia, and I was in N.Y., so we couldn't get together. During this conversation he stressed his desire to visit the island, by way of the process I initiated after he had asked me to do so several years earlier. He said that no consideration "other than the desire he had to come to the island mattered anymore," and I heard a sob from the other end of the line. It was sort of dry.

A few weeks before Heberto's death, Armando Suárez Cobián sent me the request from Lourdes Gil over email from New York: Heberto was in poor health and wanted to come. I went back down the hallways with the request, insisting on Heberto's desire to come back. Someone replied to me that "he would do everything within his reach to see that it happened, and he would bring Heberto."

If culture serves to mediate with power, it should respond to this petition and bring a poet, exiled and ill, to the land of his birth to say goodbye.

Which is why I am recounting this tale. It's a debt. I don't know why now, I don't know why in November. I remembered all of it as Nina Berberova was retelling the death of Alexandr A. Blok, and I had to close her book. In our fleeting friendship there was something more than we could express through the distance and the paranoia. I have no intention of retrieving it with additional decorations: that's how it was. A few photographs, some fraternal embraces, and a final farewell dance. I don't want to extrapolate anything that couldn't exist out of this either. I have an "action" to undertake on behalf of dead poets.

Without permission Heberto Padilla entered the land of his birth, which was always the page. He entered his definitive page. For me, who had the chance to hear him read his poems, make his jokes full of political humor; who had the chance to hear his voice for the last time on the other side of the line (from that other side, against any unjust reasoning that didn't allow him to return and, from so far away, come closer); for me he's still here, of the place he never left, and to which he already returned.

III

I didn't ever want to lose that silence in his voice on the other end of the line. But we live because we're capable of forgetting. When I write about it, I feel myself losing those pieces of conversation, a cadence getting mixed

se confunde en el marasmo de lo que creo hoy sobre su voz, un tono, unas palabras, un recuerdo intercalado entre lo que supongo de su voz y el ritmo de sus poemas, ahora. Todavía siento miedo de haber olvidado aquella voz, de estar aprendiendo, cada día que pasa, a olvidar. No haber dicho esto que sucedió entre nosotros, esa petición suya de un deseo de regresar, no de manera permanente, pero sí de manera consciente, es el principio de un olvido siniestro. Y un deseo insatisfecho crea una retórica, una permanencia. Un olvido insatisfecho crea un dolor poroso que se vuelve traición. No quiero traicionar a los poetas muertos que viven ahora en los anaqueles. ¿Qué importancia tiene el tiempo que pretendiera estar en los libreros o en las metáforas? El tiempo de un poeta cabe en un vaso de agua que se bebe "de golpe". No existe un tiempo "del afuera" o "del adentro". El tiempo de un poeta cubre una época, la extensión de una sola línea, de una sola pasión.

Cada uno debe elegir el lugar que quiere llevarse de contrabando. Volver era para Heberto Padilla constatar una presencia suya, ajena ya, borrosa, en la isla afuera. Otra metáfora. Porque la isla estaba adentro, y en esa cuadrícula de tierra que se lleva sin querer en un bolsillo o en la cartera dentro de un saquito miserable como amuleto, está enterrado su corazón. Mientras J. Brodsky buscaba un cementerio para Anna Ajmátova allá, en San Petersburgo y hacía trámites (siempre esos engorrosos trámites para sacar o depositar una sensación, un cuerpo, un poeta), nosotros todavía ni siquiera sospechábamos, más que "literariamente", lo que era pedir clemencia, acostumbrarnos a pedir clemencia, entrada, abrigo, un sitio para descansar.

¡Qué vanidad la nuestra! ¡Qué lujo, pedir!

La muerte se nos adelantó.

up in the paralysis of what I'm thinking today about his voice, a tone, some words; a memory interspersed between what I imagine to be his voice, and now the rhythm of his poems. I'm still afraid I've forgotten that voice, afraid I'm learning with every passing day how to forget. Not to speak of this thing that happened between us, his request made out of a desire to return, not permanently but in a conscious way, is the beginning of a sinister forgetting. And an unsatisfied desire creates a rhetoric, a permanence. An unsatisfied forgetting creates a porous form of sorrow, which turns into betrayal. I don't want to betray the dead poets who now live on the shelves. What importance is there to the amount of time one may have tried to occupy bookcases or metaphors? A poet's moment fits inside a glass of water that you can down as a shot. There is no time "outside" or "inside." A poet's moment covers an era, the expanse of a single line, a single passion.

Each should choose the place to which he wants to arrive as contraband. Returning was, for Heberto Padilla, the verification of his presence, already foreign, blurry, on the island outside. Another metaphor. Because the island was inside, and his heart is buried in the plot of ground that one carries around unconsciously, in a pocket or a wallet, inside a miserable jacket, like an amulet. As J. Brodsky sought a cemetery for Anna Akhmatova over there, in Saint Petersburg, and went through the procedures (always those aggravating procedures, to pick up or drop off a sensation, a body, a poet), we still didn't even suspect, except "literarily," what it meant to ask for clemency, what it meant to accustom ourselves to petitioning for clemency, for entrance, shelter, a resting place.

What vanity is ours! What a luxury, to request!

Death got there before we did.

Un cementerio para ella

Cuenta Joseph Brodsky en su entrevista con Salomón Vólkov sobre la Ajmátova, que ella ya estaba muy fría en la iglesia de San Nicolás, y él buscaba todavía, sin encontrar, un cementerio. El miedo les impedía aún a algunos dar el permiso para su entierro, entregar un pedazo de tierra municipal o hasta cerca de Finlandia donde quedaran sus huesos, después que, luego del tercer infarto, la gran poeta rusa cayera sobre la primavera. También dice Brodsky, en ese libro de entrevistas al que dedicara cinco años de su vida, que los diez y seis dibujos que Modigliani le hiciera a la Ajmátova, unos soldados se los fumaron como pitillos. Así que a ella, "la dama", "la reina de todas las Rusias", "la reina errante" como la llamara Marina Tsvietáieva, instalada en un pequeño desván junto a una cocina durante sus últimos días, le tocaba esperar, sin un funeral a su altura, un lugar para la resurrección.

Desde entonces, la he buscado en malas traducciones, en reducidos plaquettes o en cementerios sin lápidas, donde se entierra gran parte de la memoria rusa. Estuve en San Petersburgo, hace once años Leningrado. Entré a las iglesias donde oficiaban con inciensos raros las viejecillas, y caminé junto al Neva congelado. Quería encontrar un amor perdido y tener al fin, los libros de Anna Ajmátova. Pero sólo encontré, como profetiza un verso suyo, "un polvoroso solar cerca del cementerio" y allí, una definición hecha con sangre mezclada con tierra. Su poema 23 ["No soy de aquellos que abandonaron . . ."], de julio de 1922, parece escrito con sangre. La sangre que no resbala, es porosa, coagulada, espesa y tan líquida a la vez, que salta, y ya no se puede detener, mancha. Sus tonos son ocres como la sangre seca. Tan paradójicos como la sangre machando los sufijos, la armonía de un dolor, esa sonoridad del alma rusa, una resina. Una aceptación. El dolor tiene como justificación final, la llegada a un cementerio que se halla tras la puerta de algunas palabras. Un cementerio para el que ella inventó su metro, con la claridad de un pedazo de tierra suyo, cuya exactitud y apropiación logró, cortando trozos de hielo, y no se separó jamás de allí.

En su primer libro, *La tarde*, aparece este otro poema, "Rey de ojos grises". Lo escogí porque con esta fábula aparentemente sencilla, contada en catorce versos, se ve toda la vida rusa de un matrimonio vulgar cuya excepción es el susurro del álamo, el azar, la traición. Y la traición es un color gris. La Ajmátova resume con precisión, esa imposibilidad suya de hallar otra cosa que no sea la muerte "de ella" por la desaparición "de él". El deseo, la muerte, su binomio preferido. Aquí

A Cemetery for Her

In his interview with Solomon Volkov, Joseph Brodsky shares a story about Akhmatova: that her body had already grown cold in Saint Nicholas church as he searched unsuccessfully for a cemetery. Fear still kept some people from giving permission for her burial, from providing a piece of municipal ground for her bones, or even allowing a plot near Finland, after the great Russian poet collapsed in the spring that followed her third heart attack. In this book of interviews, to which he would dedicate five years of his life, Brodsky also describes the fate of sixteen drawings made of Akhmatova by Modigliani: soldiers smoked them like cigarettes. So she, "the lady," "queen of all Russias," a *reina errante* or "wandering sovereign" as Marina Tsvetaeva called her, the woman who spent her final days lying in a small attic near a kitchen, would have to wait up there without a funeral for a place of resurrection.

I've searched for her ever since in bad translations, small chapbooks, and cemeteries without gravestones where much Russian memory is buried. I was in Saint Petersburg, still called Leningrad eleven years ago. I went into the churches where the elderly women celebrated with unfamiliar incense, and I walked next to the frozen Neva. I wanted to find a lost love and hold, once and for all, Anna Akhmatova's books. But I only found—as one of her lines foretells—"a dusty plot of land by the cemetery" and there, a definition made by mixing blood with earth. It's as though her Poem 23 ["I am not with those who abandoned their land . . ."], from July 1922, were written in blood. Blood that doesn't slide, is porous, coagulated, thick and yet so liquid, blood that leaps, can no longer be held back, stains. Her tones are ochre as blood after it dries. Paradoxical as blood spotting the suffixes, the sorrow's harmony, the sonority of the Russian soul, a resin. An embrace. As its final justification the sorrow arrives at a cemetery, found behind the door of certain words. A cemetery for the quality she invented in her meter, with the clarity of a patch of earth, whose precision and appropriation she achieved by cutting pieces of ice, and never left.

In her first book, *Evening*, another poem called "Gray-eyed King" appears. I have focused on it because in this apparently simple legend, told in fourteen lines, one sees the entire Russian life of an everyday matrimony, whose exception comes in the cedar's whisper, chance, betrayal. And betrayal is a shade of gray. With precision Akhmatova summarizes her inability to find something different, something that would not be "her" death through "his" disappearance. Desire, death, her

está su fábula atravesada por la suspicacia de lo que esconde, aquel "otro" restablecido en los ojos de la niña. Este poema que parece escrito ayer en la tarde es de 1910. Sereno, preciso, tiene la violencia contenida de las mujeres rusas de ayer, de hoy. Tiene una actualidad mordaz. La muerte está del otro lado del paisaje nevado de unos ojos grises, esperando oculta para arrasar todo consuelo, todo amor. No es un poema triste, es un poema de venganza, de una venganza callada. La sospecha del marido, su crueldad, su regocijo, y la defensa de ella, con fruto. Por debajo del ritmo hay una canción. Los poemas de la Ajmátova son canciones. Los escuché en ruso una vez, me los leyeron muy de cerca, una noche. Había un tabique, otra lengua, un deseo contenido, también. Cuando las mujeres van a morir, cantan. Tengo mezclados estos versos entre una voz de hombre que se aleja, y una de mujer con gravedad serena que se queda.

Rey de ojos grises

¡Gloria a ti, dolor inconsolable!
Ayer murió el rey de ojos grises.

En la tarde otoñal sofocante y púrpura,
mi esposo regresó y dijo con calma:

"¿Sabes?, lo trajeron de la cacería . . .
Encontraron su cuerpo junto a un viejo roble.

¡Me da pena la reina, la pobre, tan joven . . . !
En una sola noche blanquearon sus cabellos."

Tomó su pipa de la chimenea
y salió a su trabajo nocturno.

Y yo fui y desperté a mi hija
y miré en sus ojos grises.

Bajo mi ventana susurraba al álamo:
"Ya no pisa la tierra tu rey . . ."

11 de diciembre de 1910
Tsárskoye Seló

favorite binomial. Here her legend is shot through with the suspicion of something it hides: that "other" reestablished in a girl's eyes. This poem, which looks as though it could have been written yesterday afternoon, is from 1910. Serene, precise, it has the contained violence of Russian women yesterday, today. It has a caustic contemporaneity. Death is just on the other side of the snowy landscape with gray eyes, waiting hidden to wipe away all consolation, all love. It's not a sad poem but a poem of vengeance, a quiet vengeance. The suspicion of the husband, his cruelty, his rejoicing, and her defense, with fruit. Under the rhythm is a song. Akhmatova's poems are songs. I heard them in Russian once; people read them to me one night with care. There was a thin wall, another language, and a contained desire. When women are going to die, they sing. I hear these lines blending the voice of a man, who is moving away, with the voice of a woman, serene and serious, who stays.

The Gray-Eyed King

Hail to thee, everlasting pain!
The gray-eyed king died yesterday.

Scarlet and close was the autumn eve,
My husband, returning, said calmly to me:

"They brought him back from the hunt, you know,
They found his body near the old oak.

Pity the queen. So young! . .
Overnight her hair has turned gray."

Then he found his pipe on the hearth
And left, as he did every night, for work.

I will wake my little daughter now,
And look into her eyes of gray.

And outside the window the poplars whisper:
"Your king is no longer on this earth . . ."

11 December 1910   91
Tsarskoye Selo

Poema 23 [No soy de aquellos que abandonaron]

No soy de aquellos que abandonaron
su tierra al destrozo enemigo.
Prefiero no escuchar sus torpes lisonjas
ni darles a ellos mis canciones.

Igual me duele la suerte del desterrado
que la de un prisionero o la de un enfermo.
Cuán oscuro es tu camino, viajero,
por tierras donde el pan tiene ese regusto a ajenjo.

Y aquí, entre el denso humo de este incendio
arruinamos nuestra menguante juventud.
Pero ni un solo golpe procuramos
desviar de los que iban dirigidos a nuestra frente.

Cuando hayan pasado los años, tardíamente,
hallarán su justificación todas estas horas . . .
No hay en este mundo gentes menos dadas al llanto,
más altivas y a la vez más simples que nosotros.

julio de 1922
Petersburgo

Poem 23 [I am not with those who abandoned their land]

I am not with those who abandoned their land
To the lacerations of the enemy.
I am deaf to their coarse flattery,
I won't give them my songs.

But to me the exile is forever pitiful,
Like a prisoner, like someone ill.
Dark is your road, wanderer,
Like wormwood smells the bread of strangers.

But here, in the blinding smoke of the conflagration
Destroying what's left of youth,
We have not deflected from ourselves
One single stroke.

And we know that in the final accounting,
Each hour will be justified . . .
But there is no people on earth more tearless
More simple and more full of pride.

July 1922
Petersburg

Como Tolstoi narra en *Resurrección*

Como Tolstoi narra en *Resurrección*, los pies del acusado al entrar en la audiencia marcan el número de pasos, el veredicto. Y si los pasos son exactos, el dolor de estómago cesará. Fallé al contar los pasos, y por eso el error me impulsó al vacío. Vuelvo a contar (acostumbrada a los relojes de ajedrecistas), qué pieza saltaré, qué espacio, qué escalón. El espejo del salón se empaña. Es tela de azogue averiada que de tanto fingir no se puede tocar. El país, el hombre, lo real. Siempre con intermediarios, dudosos. No sé hacer trampas, aunque he querido. Cuando tanteo los pasos que dar, siempre pienso en caer antes de adelantar. Pienso en retroceder, pero ni de eso soy capaz.

En el tablero puse malos ojos, malas combinaciones. Sonsaqué al azar y ahora, sólo noticias mensajeras de lo malo, de "lo peorcito" que haya, llegarán. Aunque, antes de avanzar por la calle Obispo, me sentía heredera de un paisaje como fin, con un arma poderosa y única para cuestionarse (el cetro de Antonin), pero sin esa fe suya, ¿qué hago aquí?

Frunzo el ceño y no dejo nada que contar. Alabanzas no sé, interrupciones. Malos dados, jugué. Corazones salteados en paqueticos plásticos. Los masco, sin acontecimientos, pura manía de ser normal, pero la fresa arde porque está vencida (como lo demás) y del susto a no saber, a no sentir, retrocedo como el acusado que sabe de antemano el veredicto.

No habrá resurrección, porque creímos.

As Tolstoy Recounts in *Resurrection*

As Tolstoy recounts in *Resurrection*, the feet of the accused entering court score the number of steps, the verdict. And if the steps are exact, the ache in his stomach will cease. I lost count of my steps, and that mistake propelled me into the void. I begin counting again (accustomed to timers used by chess players): over what piece will I jump, what space, what rung. The mirror in the salon grows tarnished. It's a quicksilver fabric, damaged, which can't be touched after so much dissembling. The country, the man, the real. Always through intermediaries, dubious. I don't know how to set traps, though I've wanted to. When I try to guess which steps to take, I always imagine I fall down before advancing. I consider retreating but am not even capable of that.

I laid disapproving eyes on the board, inadvisable combinations. I extracted things at random and now only the signs of bad news, the "grungy" little things, will come. Before advancing down Obispo, Bishop Street, I felt like the heir to a landscape as an end, with a unique and powerful weapon in the asking of questions (Antonin's scepter); but without his faith what am I doing here?

I wrinkle my brow and leave nothing more to tell. I don't know how to sing praises, interruptions. I threw bad rolls, I made my plays. Salted hearts in plastic packets. I chew them over without events, a pure obsession with a normal existence, but the strawberry burns because it spoiled (like the others) and in my fright at not knowing, not sensing, I retreat, like the accused who knows the verdict in advance.

There will be no resurrection, because we once believed.

In 1989, Martin Majoor designed a groundbreaking serif typeface, FF Scala, for the Vredenburg Music Center in Utrecht. In 1991, FontFont released the face as FF Scala. It appears in this book, along with its sans serif version for titles.